T
POWER
AND
INFLUENCE
OF A
WOMAN

D1371634

THE
POWER
AND
INFLUENCE
OF A
WOMAN

DR. KINGSLEY FLETCHER

Unless otherwise indicated, all Scripture quotations are taken from the Holy Bible, *New International Version,* © 1973, 1978, 1984 by the International Bible Society. Scripture quotations marked (KJV) are taken from the authorized King James Version of the Bible.

THE POWER AND INFLUENCE OF A WOMAN

Kingsley Fletcher Ministries
P.O. Box 12017
Research Triangle Park, NC 27709-2017
Ph: 919-382-1944 Fax: 919-382-3360
www.kfmlife.org

ISBN 1-880809-19-2
Printed in the United States of America
© 2003 by Kingsley Fletcher

Legacy Publishers International
1301 South Clinton Street
Denver, CO 80247
www.legacypublishersinternational.com

Cover design by: Nikki Braun

No part of this book may be reproduced or transmitted in any form or by any means, electronic or mechanical, including photocopying, recording, or by any information storage and retrieval system, without permission in writing from the publisher.

1 2 3 4 5 6 7 8 9 10 11 / 09 08 07 06 05 04 03

CONTENTS

CHAPTER 1

WOMAN, YOUR TIME HAS COME!

*If the first woman God ever made was strong enough
to turn the world upside down all alone, these women
together ought to be able to turn it back and get it
right-side up again. And now that they are asking to
do it the men better let them.*

Sojourner Truth

Once a slave and then a fiery abolitionist, Sojourner
Truth was a "figure of imposing physique, riveting
preacher and spellbinding singer who dazzled listeners
with her wit and originality. Straight-talking and unsenti-
mental, Truth became a national symbol for strong black
women—indeed, for all strong women. Like Harriet Tubman and Frederick Douglass, she is regarded as a radical
of immense and enduring influence; yet, unlike them,
what is remembered of her consists more of myth than of
personality. She was a complex woman who was born
into slavery and died a legend. Inspired by religion,
Truth transformed herself from a domestic servant
named Isabella into an itinerant pentecostal preacher;
her words of empowerment have inspired black women
and poor people the world over to this day."[1]

In 1851, Sojourner Truth gave her famous "Ain't I a Woman?" speech at the Women's Rights Convention in Akron, Ohio:

Sojourner pointed to one of the ministers. "That man over there says that women need to be helped into carriages, and lifted over ditches, and to have the best place everywhere. Nobody helps *me* any best place. *And ain't I a woman?*"

Sojourner raised herself to her full height. "Look at me! Look at my arm." She bared her right arm and flexed her powerful muscles. "I have plowed, I have planted and I have gathered into barns. And no man could head me. *And ain't I a woman?*"

"I could work as much, and eat as much as man— when I could get it—and bear the lash as well! *And ain't I a woman? I* have borne children and seen most of them sold into slavery, and when I cried out with a mother's grief, none but Jesus heard me. *And ain't I a woman?*"

The women in the audience began to cheer wildly.

She pointed to another minister. "He talks about this thing in the head. What's that they call it?"

"Intellect," whispered a woman nearby.

"That's it, honey. What's intellect got to do with women's rights or black folks' rights? If my cup won't hold but a pint and yours holds a quart, wouldn't you be mean not to let me have my little half-measure full?"

"That little man in black there! He says women can't have as much rights as men. 'Cause Christ wasn't a woman." She stood with outstretched arms and eyes of fire. "Where did your Christ come from?"

"Where did your Christ come from?", she thundered again. "From God and a Woman! Man had nothing to do with him!"

The entire church now roared with deafening applause.

"If the first woman God ever made was strong enough to turn the world upside down all alone, these women together ought to be able to turn it back and get it right-side up again. And now that they are asking to do it the men better let them."[2]

Women of God, your time has come! I believe God wants to provoke women and cause them to see what God sees about them, to accept what God knows about them and to walk in what God has ordained for them. This book is going to touch your life and the lives of those you influence through your family, your job, your ministry and your relationships. You are going to come into the realization that God has a divine plan for your life and you are going to walk in it!

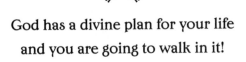

**God has a divine plan for your life
and you are going to walk in it!**

In fact, it is going to be dangerous to hear and to accept what God has said about you. God is going to make you very uncomfortable if you choose not to walk into your divine destiny. So get ready, woman of God—YOUR TIME HAS COME!

A Repressed Woman

It is amazing how tradition, stereotypes and history have demeaned the importance and value of women in this nation and around the world. In many places, there is still the need to elevate the status of women, to help them gain their equality and freedom, and to provide them with basic human and civil rights such as voting and education.

The world has steered very far away from what God intended when He created men and women. The world has decided that because men are bigger, that also must make them smarter and more qualified to lead; however, that is untrue.

The Church has misused Scripture and taken Bible verses out of context to validate the elimination of women from key roles in the church. Although God clearly used powerful and anointed women of God in the Old

The world has decided that because men are bigger,

that also must make them smarter and more

qualified to lead; however, that is untrue.

Testament and the New Testament to impact His Kingdom, the Church has incorrectly used a few Scriptures to silence women. The traditionally male-dominated pastorate has effectively misused and misquoted the words of the apostle Paul where he says that women are to learn in silence (see 1 Cor. 15:34). What is often omitted is the historical context of the that particular culture and time, as well as the original Greek meanings that have been (mis)translated over the centuries. Paul's ministry was deeply impacted by women—several of whom he addressed in his letters to the various churches in the New Testament. Paul greeted female believers as "those who labored with me in the gospel," and "my fellow workers" (see Rom. 16:3; Phil. 4:3). It is time for us to correct the errors of the past regarding the role of women.

History and tradition have also been major culprits in restricting the religious and spiritual activities of women. Society and socialization have had a major impact on how women and men are reared differently and forced into stereotypical gender roles. Even today, psychological studies of new parents show that they tend to treat baby boys and baby girls differently during the infant and toddler years. Boys are described with words such as "smart, alert and attentive," while girls are described as, "cute, pretty, adorable and precious."

Little boys are encouraged to be strong and adventurous, while girls are told to "sit down and act like a lady." Little boys are shaped and molded to become leaders, while our girls have been trained to "get a husband." Young men have been sent to college to get an education and find a job so they can support a family. Women have been taught only to cook, sew and support their husbands. The end result is that women have not been trained or prepared to be effective leaders in our society because their rights and responsibilities have been taken away. And in many cases, a woman is not prepared to survive if her husband passes away or abandons the family.

Our society has changed and become demoralized. The institutions of marriage and family have deteriorated. Mothers are raising children alone and a large number of them are on welfare or living in poverty because they have not been trained or prepared to survive on their own. The problem with simply "getting a husband" and trusting that a man will take care of you is that nowadays marriages don't last. Men are not fulfilling their godly duties to seek first the Kingdom of God and to love their wives like Christ loves the Church. So if women aren't prepared to make it on their own, the entire family suffers.

Both men and women need to understand that God is first. Your ultimate trust and faith must be in God, and the foremost relationship must be with Jesus Christ. God created men and women to reign and rule as equals. So it is not fair that men have dominated and controlled women, or that society has stripped women of their rights.

My wife and I have two daughters. We see the inequities that exist in society, and we are raising our daughters to put their trust in God—not in a man who may fail them, or in a society that may abuse and disregard them. Our daughters know who they are in Christ and how they should be treated. They know that they are intelligent and powerful, influential young women whom God has destined for success. We owe it to our daughters—as believers—to prepare them mentally, spiritually and emotionally for the world that awaits them. Our young women must know who they are and what they are capable of accomplishing through Christ.

It is unfair to isolate half of the population and neglect them of their God-given ability to survive, to instruct and to lead. I believe God wants to restore the purpose and equality in which He created men and women. The time has come for women to stand up and be counted. God has called women to do a great work for Him, and there is no tradition, stereotype or man that can stop the plan of God for a woman's life. Woman of God, your time has come.

GOD BLESSED *THEM*

Then God said, "Let us make man in our image, in our likeness, and let them rule over the fish of the sea and the birds of the air, over the livestock, over all the earth, and over all the creatures that move along the ground" (Genesis 1:26).

God has called woman to do a great work for Him,

and there is no tradition, stereotype or man that

can stop the plan of God for a woman's life.

It's interesting to observe what God actually said: "Let us make man in our image, in our likeness, and let *them*...." He started with "Let us," and He said what He wanted to do. Then He said, "...let *them* rule over the fish of the sea." He didn't say, "...let *him* rule." The Word says, "Let *them* rule"—or have dominion over—according to other translations. "So God created man in his own image, in the image of God he created him; male and female he created *them*" (Gen. 1:27, emphasis added).

"God blessed *them* and said to *them*" (Gen. 1:28a, emphasis added). He did not only speak to the man—He spoke to both of them. "He blessed them and said to them." God did not speak before He blessed. He blessed, then He spoke. That shows us anything that God has created He has already blessed. So not only do we have what the Word says, we also have an example of what God has done.

God knew that for a man to actually live a fruitful and productive life, he needed the assistance of a woman. When God put Adam in a deep sleep, He took one of his ribs and formed Eve. So men and women were created from the same source. Whatever is in a man is also in a woman. Adam called Eve, "bone of my bones, and flesh of my flesh" (see Gen. 2:23). Men and women are one; they are designed to complete each other, to help each other and to support each other.

We are all blessed of God; whether you are male or female, you are blessed of God. We are blessed of God in spite of our gender. We are blessed of God in spite of our color or ethnicity. We are blessed of God in spite of our status and stature. We are blessed of God.

God blessed them and He said, "Be fruitful and increase in number; fill the earth and subdue it" (Gen. 2:28a). He spoke to the two of them, both male and female. He said, "You have to fill the earth and subdue it." Now if this Scripture is true and this Scripture is believed by the Church, then we have to look at this very seriously because it appears that, over time, men have been exalted into superior positions and omitted the role and significance of women in fulfilling God's commands.

Even saved men who know the Word of God have been guilty of objectifying women, since that is what we have been socialized to do. When I first got married, I wanted my wife to do everything I told her to do. She was a quiet and meek woman, and I thought she would just jump whenever I told her to. But as we both continued to learn and grow in Christ, I realized that she wasn't just going to do everything I said; she had a mind and will of her own. Try as I might, she was not going to be pushed around and told what to do. If I wanted to be happily married, I was going to have to submit to her as much as I wanted her to submit to me.

Now, she will do anything I ask her to do...because I will do anything she asks me to do. We are equal. We are one. We submit to each other, and, as a result, we have become one flesh. When you are one, there is no control or domination. There is no subjection; there is equal submission. There is unity and purpose.

Our God is a God of purpose. When He created males and females, He created them with a purpose in mind. God—who made man and woman—gave each one of us the opportunity to experience the joys of life during various times and seasons. Those who understand purpose also understand the importance and significance of time and season.

Since creation, you have been instructed to "be fruitful and multiply"; to subdue the earth. Your life was designed to bear fruit. Jesus cursed the fig tree for not producing fruit—it didn't fulfill its purpose. The unfulfilled life is a cursed life. The time has come for every man and every woman to evaluate his or her life and seek to understand their purpose. We are all accountable for using our God-given talents and abilities in the manner that best glorifies God. The time has long since passed for women to step up to the tasks at hand and walk in their God-given authority as leaders in Christ.

The Appointed Time for a Woman

Historically, men have been placed in natural and spiritual leadership roles, and this standard has been perpetuated since the beginning of mankind. Traditionally some men have been called to the role of leaders—even if they're not qualified to lead. Consequently, men have been acknowledged and honored for their leadership even when someone else does the work. Men have been placed first, even if it has meant sacrificing or neglecting the contributions of others—especially women.

But the time has come when women will not have to fight to be heard or accepted anymore. The time has come where it is going to become very evident that the

Church we know today has been raised and built on the backs of women. Women are givers. They understand the law of seed time and harvest time, and they pay tithes to honor God and protect their households. Women are prayer warriors. Men will stand and speak at great length, but it is women who will humble themselves and bow in prayer—taking authority over the enemy in the name of Jesus. It is women who weep and wail for the souls of their children. It is women who travail in prayer until they give birth to their God-given vision.

It is women who protect and nurture their sons and daughters and raise them according to the Word of God. It is women who fill the church pews on Sunday mornings and the prayer benches on Wednesday evenings; who stay up all night long in prayer interceding for lost husbands and lost children. Women have been used mightily by God, and the world will now see and recognize their contributions.

In the fourth chapter of the Book of John, there is a story about a Samaritan woman who lived a very sinful life. Her life was not hidden; as a matter of fact, it was well-known. The Bible says that one day this woman went to draw water from a well that had been dug by their father, Jacob. Jesus met this lady at the well, and they started conversing. Jesus asked her for water and she told Him, "We have nothing in common." She said, "I am a Samaritan and You are a Jew." In their dialogue Jesus said to her, "I have a gift for you, and if you really knew what kind of gift I have for you, you would gladly give Me to drink because what I am going to give you has eternal life." In their conversation Jesus went further to talk about something that was very personal to this woman. He said, "Go and get Me your husband." This woman had enjoyed the company of five men and she was living with the sixth one—who wasn't her husband. She was a woman who provided pleasure for sinful men; she was the delight of loose and irresponsible men.

Recognizing this woman's purpose and significance, Jesus made a simple statement that eventually changed the life of this woman forever. The woman's response to Him changed from, "I don't have water to give You" to "Sir, I perceive that You are the Christ." From that moment, not only had her life changed, but others' as well. She had encountered the living Word of God and told everyone in town, "Come and see a man who told me everything I have ever done. This man I perceive is the Christ." Apparently Jesus knew from the time He met the woman at the well, that it was the appointed time and season in her life for her to begin her purpose for living. He met her at that point. There is always a time and a season, and there is always a place for every man or every woman to fulfill their purpose. What is God trying to tell you at this time and season in your life?

Don't let this time and this season pass you by. This is the time, this is the season and this is the place where God wants to change your life. You will be able to walk out of your current situation, leave your past behind, and prove to the world that you are a woman with purpose and a woman with a divine destiny.

A FREE WOMAN

God has been preparing you for this moment in time. He has given you visions. God has given you revelations. God has been giving you a word for your family, and you are holding your family together by the prophetic word of the Lord. You may be saying, "I don't think God will ever use me." I am here to tell you, not only does He want to use you, but He wants to use you mightily to accomplish His will on earth.

Women, don't quit, because the favor of God is upon you. Don't ever believe that you cannot excel because you are in a man's world. You are in God's world, and God made man and woman. The time has come to cease being silent because someone told you years ago that women cannot speak out for God. The time has come for you to be free to serve God. The world may misuse the word *freedom*, but you, as a child of God, use your freedom to serve Him and to bless many. You are a free woman of God because when you accepted Jesus—the same way man accepted Him—He made you free in Him...and you are free indeed.

God wants His children to be free in Him. Liberated women are those who have been set free by the power of God and the anointing of the Holy Spirit. There are several distinguishing characteristics of liberated women:

- Liberated women know who they are in Christ.
- Liberated women seek to please God.
- Liberated women know they have value and purpose.
- Liberated women are free from the opinions of others.

19

- Liberated women do not seek the approval of men.
- Liberated women walk boldly in their calling.
- Liberated women are free to express their emotions.
- Liberated women are free to praise and worship God.
- Liberated women are open and available to be used by God.
- Liberated women will not allow themselves to be dominated or controlled.
- Liberated women understand destiny.

"Where the Spirit of the Lord is, there is liberty" (2 Cor. 3:17 KJV). "Now the Lord is the Spirit, and where the Spirit of the Lord is, there is freedom" (2 Cor. 3:17).

Even in this day and age, there are places where women are still being oppressed and have yet to gain their freedom. They aren't allowed to be educated, they aren't allowed to speak in certain places, and in public they remain several paces behind a man. But this is not what God intended. He created them male and female to equally rule and subdue the earth.

We can help each other, we can lead each other, and we can inspire each other—but we cannot control each other. The Bible instructs us to submit ourselves one to another (see Eph. 5:21). When there is equal submission, there is no dominance or control; but when there is no free will or submission, it becomes oppressive and controlling. There is something inherently wrong with trying to dominate and control each other because Jesus Christ

Himself came to set the captive free. "If the Son therefore shall make you free, you shall be free indeed" (Jn. 8:36 KJV). No person can obtain true freedom until the freedom giver is in his or her life. And when you are free in Jesus, when you are liberated by the Holy Spirit, there is nothing you cannot do.

The world has robbed you, and the enemy has robbed you. The world has lied to you, and the enemy has lied to you. Men have lied to you, and even you have begun to believe those lies. But God is not as a man, and

There is something inherently wrong with trying

to dominate and control each other because

Jesus Christ Himself came to set the captive free.

He cannot lie. Whose report shall you believe? Believe in the report of the Lord. He created you fearfully and wonderfully in His image. He has called you to teach, to preach and to lead others to Christ. Stand up and take your place in the Kingdom of God. Woman, your time has come!

ENDNOTES
    1. Duane Bristow, "Sojourner Truth." *Duane & Eva's Old Kentucky Home Page on the Web.* Copyright 1995. July 4, 2001. June 5, 2003. <www.webcom. com/duane/truth.html>.
    2. Ibid.

CHAPTER 2

THE ROLE OF A WOMAN

Everything birthed in the natural and in the spiritual comes from a woman. Eve—the first woman to grace the earth—means "life giver." From the beginning of the creation of the world until now, it has been a woman's role to "bring life to things" and to give birth physically, spiritually and emotionally.

I am going to say something that may shock you because you rarely hear this message being taught. It has often been said that the man is the head of the household. That is true because the Bible says so. But there is a distinct difference between who is the head of the household and who is spiritual in the household. It takes a godly man to be the leader of his home. But if a man has forfeited his spiritual responsibility by not accepting Christ or not submitting to the will of God, does he still qualify to be the spiritual head of the house? No.

WHO IS THE SPIRITUAL HEAD OF THE HOUSE?

It is the one who has a relationship with God who brings protection to the family, and, in many instances, that individual is a woman. Until a man makes a commitment to the Lord and submits his life to the lordship of

Jesus Christ, he does not qualify to hear and receive the blessings of God for his household. God will not impart His will and His desire to a man who doesn't serve Him or to a man who has not developed a listening ear to hear what the Spirit of God has to say. God will speak to the woman—the spiritual head of the household—until the man steps into his rightful place in Christ.

It is the one who has a relationship with God
who brings protection to the family, and, in many
instances, that individual is a woman.

So many women are trapped in marriages and missing out on the blessings of God because they're waiting for the man—the head of the household—to step into his assigned role. Unfortunately, if the man isn't qualified for spiritual leadership, the woman and the entire household suffers. It is for this reason that the Word warns us to not be unequally yoked with unbelievers—in marriage, in relationships or in business. Just as important, two saved individuals can be unequally yoked if either of them are out of God's will for their lives and not in the proper place God desires them to be.

Do not mistake or misunderstand God's desire for order. He has indeed called men to be the head within the house; that means men are accountable for what happens within their home. In the Garden of Eden, even though the serpent approached Eve and persuaded her to eat from the tree of the knowledge of good and evil, God required a response from Adam. It is Adam who was accountable because God expects and requires order. But women of God, please do not misplace your spiritual gifts or deny the word that God has given to you because you're waiting on your unsaved husband to impart godly wisdom into your household. If you have the gift of spiritual leadership, God may want to use you to inspire your husband to walk into his divine calling. God may want to use your gifts and your talents to bring your husband into salvation. Do not deny the evident power of God in your life because you're a woman.

THE SPIRITUAL DISCERNMENT OF A WOMAN

There is a time, there is a season and there is a place for every man and every woman. According to Second Kings 4:8-10: "One day Elisha went to Shunem. And a well-to-do woman was there, who urged him to stay for a meal. So whenever he came by, he stopped there to eat. She said to her husband, 'I know that this man who often comes our way is a holy man of God.' Let's make a small room on the roof and put in it a bed and a table, a chair and a lamp for him. Then he can stay there whenever he comes to us.' "

This Shunammite (refers to male or female) was a woman who had wealth, means and influence. This woman was married and well-to-do, and she had a position and a spiritual gift that her husband did not have. She recognized the man of God and put herself and her household in a position to receive the blessings of God.

In our culture, if a woman has wealth and is secure, or if a woman has a position higher than her husband, she will either be considered a bossy woman or a woman who has no regard for her home and will sacrifice her home for her success. This is simply not true.

The woman from Shunem was an example of what we would call a successful, independent woman. The Bible says she used her generosity to be of help to people in ministry. She was so sensitive and keen and had the grace of discernment that she could discern who was of God and who was not of God. She apparently discerned that Elisha was a man of God.

Why is it that the Shunammite woman's husband could not see or know that the man called Elisha was a man of God? How is it that the man of the house could not sense or acknowledge that the man who passed by, the man that his wife had taken upon herself to provide for, was a man of God?

This man apparently did not operate in discernment. He could not see that Elisha was a man of God. However, not only did the woman provide for the prophet, but she went to her husband and said, "Let's take it one step further. Let's not just feed the man and send him on his way. Let's make it a point that this man becomes part of our family." It's the same case today. Women have made it part of their business to make Jesus Christ a part of their family before their husbands even respond or recognize it. Apparently the husband of the Shunammite woman was very understanding because he went along with his wife's suggestion.

> *One day when Elisha came, he went up to his room and lay down there. He said to his servant Gehazi, "Call the Shunammite." So he called her, and she stood before him. Elisha said to him, "Tell her, 'You have gone to all this trouble for us. Now what can be done for you? Can we speak on your behalf to the king or the commander of the army?' " She replied, "I have a home among my own people." "What can be done for her?" Elisha asked. Gehazi said, "Well, she has no son and her husband is old." Then Elisha said, "Call her." So he called her, and she stood in the doorway. "About this time next year," Elisha said, "you will hold a son in your arms"* (2 Kings 4:11-15).

During that day and time—culturally speaking—it was considered wrong for Elisha to call for the woman and not the man because the man was supposed to be the head of the house. But the reason why Elisha did not call the man was because the one who was supposed to be the spiritual leader of the household was not qualified to hear and recognize the voice of God. Yet, Elisha saw fit to bless their family with a son anyway because of the spiritual discernment and faithfulness of the woman.

GOD USES WOMEN IN MIGHTY WAYS TOO

God has always looked at women the same way He looks at men. God will allow His blessings to come through anyone—male or female—who avails himself or herself to be an entry point for the things of God. Therefore it is fair to say that God does not look at your gender to qualify His blessings. He is a God of all flesh. He is not a God of some flesh. He is not a God of the male flesh. He is not a God of the female flesh. He is a God of *all* flesh and there is nothing too hard for God.

God will allow His blessings to come through anyone—male or female—who avails himself or herself to be an entry point for the things of God.

There is a time for every creature of God and there is a season for every man and every woman. In fact God intends for each one of us to leave a mark on our generation before we depart from this earth. I personally don't believe that a woman's role is just to bear children—and nothing more. You can do more than bear children, and you can do more than run a household. God created women to have value and to play a significant role in His plan and purpose. Do not believe the lie that society has told you for so long about a woman's place being behind a man or in the kitchen and the bedroom. A woman's place is to be where God tells her to be and to fulfill God's will for her life. To some it may sound spiritual and humbling to sit quietly while the man does a mighty work for God, but let's go back to the Word of God to find out His true plan for the woman of God.

The apostle Paul is often charged with subjecting women to secondary roles in the Church because of a few statements that have been misinterpreted and misconstrued. But when studying Scripture—especially regarding a subject as controversial as the role of women in the Church—it's important to consider the context, the original meaning, the historical setting and the current circumstances that influenced what was being said. Some excellent insight on Paul and his relationship and views on women in the Church is shared in this passage from *Every Woman in the Bible.*

> Paul was not a reformer, but a transformer. He did not challenge institutions, he challenged individuals. Paul was convinced that anyone in any situation could please God, and he encouraged believers to use whatever opportunities they had to do so. This approach to the Christian life is expressed in the general principle: "Let each one remain in the same calling in which he was called" (1 Cor. 7:20).[1]
>
> "It is shameful for women to speak in church" (1 Cor. 14:35). Two clues to the solution are found in this verse. The first is in the present infinitive ("to speak"). While the Greek word *speak* does not indicate any specific kind of speech, the present infinitive *portrays continual speaking up.* These women continually, repeatedly, and disruptively spoke out in church meetings.
>
> The second clue is "let them ask their own husbands at home, for it is shameful for gunaikin (women or wives) to speak in church." This tells us that the word rendered "women" in 14:35 should be translated "wives." It is far more natural in this context to understand Paul

to be speaking of the wives of husbands mentioned rather than of all women.

These two clues suggest that the specific problem in Corinth involved certain wives (not all women) creating chaos by repeatedly and inappropriately speaking up in church gatherings.[2]

This text provides an insightful perspective as to how the words of Paul have been twisted and turned to suit the desires of men. However, it is evident that the role of women has been and always will be significant in the Church. God wants to use those who avail themselves to Him—regardless of gender.

WAS PAUL REALLY TALKING ABOUT SUBORDINATION?

"The head of every man is Christ, the head of woman is man, and the head of Christ is God" (1 Cor. 11:3). Paul launched this teaching with a strong affirmation. Those who hold a hierarchical view of the relationship between the sexes view this as a statement about authority and subordination. They read it as if Paul had written, "Every man is under Christ's authority, woman is under man's authority, and Christ is under God's authority." This however is not what Paul wrote. While "head" in Greek may mean leader or "boss," this meaning is unusual. Even in the Greek translation of the Old Testament, in nine out of ten cases where the Hebrew Old Testament uses rosh (head) in the sense of "leader," a different Greek word than kephale (head) is chosen to translate it. Thus the argument that "head" here must mean "authority over" is hardly compelling.

Another problem exists with this interpretation...Paul is making a distinct statement about three different relationships:

- Christ is the "head" of "every man."
- The husband is the "head" of the wife.
- God is the "head" of Christ.

"Head" in this passage cannot be used here to ascribe superiority or subordination; Christ is not inferior to God the Father. "Head" cannot mean that men are "the source" of women, for husbands are not the source of wives.[3]

Rather than limit women's participation by denying them significant roles, these passages were intended to correct specific situations in Corinth and in Ephesus that prevented women praying, prophesying, and teaching effectively.

Yet in all our discussion we have not mentioned one stunning affirmation found in Galatians 3:26-28. There Paul wrote: "For you are all sons of God through faith in Christ Jesus. For as many of you as were baptized into Christ have put on Christ. There is neither Jew nor Greek, there is neither slave nor free, there is neither male nor female; for you are all one in Christ Jesus."

All believers alike are lifted in Christ to the legal position held only by "sons" in Roman law. In the church all the old barriers are taken down. Whether the barrier is ethnic (Jew or Greek), social (slave vs. free), or gender-based (male vs. female), that barrier is irrelevant in the body of Christ. We are to see each other as equals now: as one in Christ Jesus.[4]

From this passage—and of course from God's Word
and His example—we see that women are called to be

The gift of leadership knows no gender.
God can use anyone who is willing
and available to hear and obey His voice.

powerful leaders: in our churches, our schools, businesses and homes. The gift of leadership knows no gender.
God can use anyone who is willing and available to hear
and obey His voice.

THE LEADERSHIP OF A WOMAN

A leader is one who will seek the best interest for
those who follow. A leader is one who provides emotional, material and spiritual guidance, and who gives wise
counsel and sets a good example.

Consider Deborah in the Old Testament who is widely known as the first woman judge in the Bible. In Judges
4 and 5, she is referred to as the "prophetess who judged
Israel." According to Scripture, Deborah was both a
prophetess and the wife of Lapidoth. Her name means
"woman of a torch-like spirit" or "woman of a fiery spirit."

Deborah was endowed with the gift of prophetic
command, and it was through her leadership and guidance that Israel was set free from 20 years of oppression
by Jabin, the king of Hazor, and his commander Sisera.

Deborah sent for Barak, son of Abinoam, who lived
in Kedesh in the land of Naphtali. She shared with Barak

that the Lord, God of Israel, was going to deliver the children of Israel from the oppression of King Jabin. She instructed Barak to assemble 10,000 men to prepare for battle at the Kishon River, and there God would deliver them.

However, so great was Deborah's influence in the land that Barak refused to go into battle—even with God's promise—unless Deborah agreed to go with him. By doing so, Barak relinquished the honor of victory in battle because Israel's deliverance was accomplished through the hands of Deborah—a woman. When Barak's army marched, Deborah marched with them, leading them to victory. God confounded the army of Sisera and left them vulnerable to Barak's attack. The majority of the army of Sisera was slain, and this mighty victory was attributed to Deborah and commemorated in her song found in Judges 5.

God also used a woman prophetess to confirm Simeon's words before his prophecy came to pass. Simeon had been called upon as a leader. The Bible says in Luke 2:25 that he was a righteous and devout man of God. It is told that Simeon was waiting for the consolation of Israel and the Holy Spirit was upon him. It had been revealed to him by the Holy Spirit that he would not die before he had seen the Lord's Christ. The Word of God says:

Moved by the Spirit, he went into the temple courts. When the parents brought in the child Jesus to do for him what the custom of the Law required, Simeon took him in his arms and praised God saying: "Sovereign

Lord, as you have promised, you now dismiss your servant in peace. For my eyes have seen your salvation, which you have prepared in the sight of all people, a light for revelation to the Gentiles and for glory to your people Israel." The child's father and mother marveled at what was said about him. Then Simeon blessed them and said to Mary his mother: "This child is destined to cause the falling and rising of many in Israel, and to be a sign that will be spoken against, so that the thoughts of many hearts will be revealed. And a sword will pierce your own soul too" (Luke 2:27-35).

But the Bible says that the prophecy wasn't going to be complete until the prophetess Anna showed up. The prophetess was one who had availed her life, had been chosen by God, and was ordained by the Holy Spirit to speak forth the word of God to His people. So God therefore did not select Simeon to be the only spokesman to confirm His word; He also appointed a prophetess to confirm what Simeon had seen. God used Anna, a single woman—with no husband or male leader—who did not have any man over her to tell her what to do but God.

Luke 2:36-37 states, "There was also a prophetess, Anna, the daughter of Phanuel, of the tribe of Asher. She was very old; she had lived with her husband seven years after her marriage, and then was a widow until she was eighty-four. She never left the temple but worshiped night and day, fasting and praying." Note that nothing was said about Simeon's relationship to the temple, but only about the woman in the temple. Is this not the same case today? Look at the temple, which is the church. Look at the ones who spend most of their time in the church—it's the women of God who stay in the temple to worship and pray.

God has called you to be a leader—maybe through ministry or as the spiritual leader in your house. You may have failed or fallen short in the past, but that is part of life. That is not a death sentence, nor is it the final act of your life. In fact, you may have let things get out of control; that does not mean you cannot have a second, third or tenth chance to begin again. It simply means that you have the ability to become smarter and wiser because of your experience. It means you have the potential to be a powerful testimony of God's grace and mercy. For too long women have stood in the background waiting for the approval of a man. But there are times when you have to let every man be a liar and let only God be true.

Look at the corporate world today. There are many women in leadership roles and powerful positions. If

**For too long women have stood in the
background waiting for the approval of a man.**

some of them had listened to the men in their lives—who said they would fail—many of them would be on welfare or living in a homeless shelter. God did not create you to settle for less, to live on a fixed income, or to wait for a man to take care of you. He called you to be a leader, a conqueror and a testimony to the miraculous power of God. He called you to be an example to others and to glorify Him. Women of God, you must know and recognize your place in God. He has called you to preach the gospel, to minister, to pray and to serve Him. Do not be disillusioned by the man in your life who is not submitted to God.

Accomplishing Great Things for God

Woman, your time has come! You are at the right place now for your life to be changed. You are at the right place now for your life to be influenced by God so that you can take your influence to the world. Honestly, mostly women are the backbone of the local church and without you, the pastors would not be effective in ministry. Women are the backbone of our families and their jobs—even though they don't give you the title you deserve. Even though they don't give you the money you deserve and they would rather have a man in your place. Your gift and your influence are beyond what you can see. Don't let anything move you away from God's plan and purpose for your life.

Don't let the opinions of others enslave you; simply trust God. After all, He is the healer of your broken heart and the restorer of your soul; the Lord shall be your shepherd and He shall hold you in His arms. He shall rock you in His arms and show you that He is the one who loves you with everlasting love. No one can take that away from you.

You are a woman of substance, influence, strength and power. Woman of God, your value is beyond what man can measure. You are a beautiful, glorious creation of God. You are the expression of His continual grace. He has sustained you until today because He knows that your work is not done and with the time God has allotted you on earth, you are going to leave a mark for your generation.

The same God who allowed the sun and the rain to bless man is the same God who made you. "Oh daughter of Zion, lift up your head and let your king come in. The king of glory comes in" (Zech. 9:9, author's paraphrase). Yes, it seems as though the struggles of life have taken their toll; but be not dismayed, God has not forgotten you.

You are a powerful and anointed woman of God. Your spirit of discernment alerts you of the plans of the enemy. Your sensitivity to the Spirit of God allows the Holy Spirit to keep moving on the earth. Your faithfulness in prayer allows God to bless His people. Your submission to God allows Him to bless you. Your petitions for others allow God to save souls.

God said that He would pour out His Spirit on *all* flesh, and His sons and daughters would prophesy. You are a daughter of Zion, and Zion is called a place of praise. You shall glorify your God and praise His holy name (see Joel 2:28-29; Zech. 2:10).

I am speaking prophetically to you in this book that whatever God has called you to accomplish in life (whether it's in ministry, in business, in being a wife or mother), you can do it in the name of Jesus. Man may not have recognized it, others may not be able to see it, and your friends may not believe it. But God says the very thing man has not seen is the very thing He will use, for out of desolation shall come bountiful blessings. Out of you and through your life shall come healing and deliverance; the joy of the Lord and victory shall go forth. You are a watchman that sits on the wall. The strength and leadership of women have protected the Church from the onslaught of the enemy. If we were to lose our women intercessors today, the Church would be invaded by the devil. Woman of God, you are responsible for holding back the forces of evil—dangers seen and unseen. You are a valuable woman of God. You see what most men cannot see, for you have discernment and you are a visionary. Your ability to see things turn around is what God will use to touch and heal our nations.

The Church must release women from the long-standing religious strongholds and allow God to do what He says He is going to do through them because in Christ Jesus there is no male or female. The Church has become a breeding ground for frustration. Many women are frustrated and have begun to question the call of God on their lives because of past stereotypes that the Church has perpetuated. Women have begun to question the times that God has spoken to them in prayer regarding the call on their life. They've begun to question their own femininity because it seems that male attributes are more acceptable in leadership roles. As a result, some women are beginning to act like men in order to pursue their calling in God. Understand this: God knew you were a woman when He called you. Your gender will not be a hindrance to the plans of God for your life. Woman, rise up in Jesus' name! Your time has come. In God there is neither male nor female; there is neither bond nor free. There is no Jew and there is no Gentile. God is not a respecter of persons, nor is He a respecter of gender. God

God knew you were a woman when
He called you. Your gender will not be a
hindrance to the plans of God for your life.

made both genders to honor Him, and He will not abandon you because you are a woman for the sake of a man who is walking in sin.

ENDNOTES

1. Sue and Larry Richards, *Every Woman in the Bible* (Nashville, TN: Thomas Nelson, 1999), 220.

2. Ibid., 225.

3. Ibid., 222.

4. Ibid., 232.

CHAPTER 3

POWER AND PERSISTENCE

Everywhere you look in Scripture you can see the faithful and committed determination of women—how they persisted in prayer and pressed their way through situations in spite of the challenges.

I am reminded of the parable of the persistent woman in Luke 18.

In a certain town there was a judge who neither feared God nor cared about men. And there was a widow in that town who kept coming to him with the plea, "Grant me justice against my adversary." For some time he refused. But finally he said to himself, "Even though I don't fear God or care about men, yet because this widow keeps bothering me, I will see that she gets justice, so that she won't eventually wear me out with her coming!" And the Lord said, "Listen to what the unjust judge says. And will not God bring about justice for his chosen ones, who cry out to him day and night? Will he keep putting them off? I tell you, he will see that they get justice, and quickly" (Luke 18:2-8a).

God—our just and righteous Judge—is listening to your plea. He is not concerned about your maleness or femaleness, for there is no gender difference regarded by God. He only wants your relationship with Him to be strengthened and your life to glorify Him.

There is also the story about the daughters of Zelophehad in the Old Testament. They are a wonderful example of progressive, intelligent women who overcame the odds against them during a time when women were considered to be property or second-class citizens. Mahlah, Noah, Hoglah, Milcah and Tirzah were the daughters of a sonless father and made a claim to their father's inheritance. The tradition was for fathers to pass down land and other inheritances to their sons. But their father, Zelophehad, had only five daughters.

Upon the passing of their father, the daughters took their complaint to Moses so that he would grant them their rightful inheritance:

> *"Our father died in the desert. He was not among Korah's followers, who banded together against the Lord, but he died for his own sin and left no sons. Why should our father's name disappear from his clan because he had no son? Give us property among our father's relatives." So Moses brought their case before the Lord and the Lord said to him, "What Zelophehad's daughters are saying is right. You must certainly give them property as inheritance among their father's relatives and turn their father's inheritance over to them"* (Numbers 27:3-7).

Once again, God's divine law overruled the societal gender-based laws that usually overlooked and discounted the significance of women.

THE TOUCH OF A WOMAN

There are times when you simply cannot take "no" for an answer. Here is an amazing story of a woman whose persistence to touch Jesus should encourage everyone who reads about her to press their way until they get the answer they need.

> *Now when Jesus returned, a crowd welcomed him, for they were all expecting him. Then a man named Jairus, a ruler of the synagogue, came and fell at Jesus' feet, pleading with him to come to his house because his only daughter, a girl of about twelve, was dying. As Jesus was on his way, the crowds almost crushed him. And a woman was there who had been subject to bleeding for twelve years, but no one could heal her. She came up behind him and touched the edge of his cloak, and immediately her bleeding stopped* (Luke 8:40-44).

There are times when you simply
cannot take "no" for an answer.

This woman with the "issue of blood" (KJV) could have just resigned herself to her illness and given up hope. She had tried time and time again, but to no avail.

She had spent years—and all her money—seeking to be healed. No one could help her. But when she heard that Jesus was in town, she mustered enough strength to press her way through the crowd to touch Him. This woman demonstrated power, persistence and perseverance.

There were men all around who stationed themselves as barricades to protect Jesus from the crowd—even preventing those who needed help from reaching Him. And although there were obstacles in the way to keep her from getting to Jesus, she knew that He alone was the answer that she needed. If she could but touch the hem of His garment, she knew she would be healed.

"Who touched me?" Jesus asked. When they all denied it, Peter said, "Master, the people are crowding and pressing against you." But Jesus said, "Someone touched me; I know that power has gone out from me." Then the woman, seeing that she could not go unnoticed, came trembling and fell at his feet. In the presence of all the people, she told why she had touched him and how she had been instantly healed. Then he said to her, "Daughter, your faith has healed you. Go in peace" (Luke 8:45-48).

Jesus knew that this wasn't just any ordinary touch. This was a touch that required the anointing, a touch that demanded His power, such that He felt virtue leave Him. This was a touch that demanded His attention. By her determination she touched Jesus and was instantly healed. What situation in your life demands the attention of the

Lord? Just reach out and touch Him—and be instantly healed.

THE FAITH OF A WOMAN

In Matthew 15, there is another instance of a woman demonstrating persistence by asking Jesus to heal her daughter vexed by demons.

> *A Canaanite woman from that vicinity came to him, crying out, "Lord, Son of David, have mercy on me! My daughter is suffering terribly from demon-possession." Jesus did not answer a word. So his disciples came to him and urged him, "Send her away, for she keeps crying out after us." He answered, "I was sent only to the lost sheep of Israel." The woman came and knelt before him. "Lord, help me!" she said. He replied, "It is not right to take the children's bread and toss it to their dogs." "Yes, Lord," she said, "but even the dogs eat the crumbs that fall from their masters' table." Then Jesus answered, "Woman, you have great faith! Your request is granted." And her daughter was healed from that very hour* (Matthew 15:22-28).

This woman was determined to get what she needed no matter the cost. She would not take no for an answer and she would not be denied. Even when Jesus tried to discourage her, she persisted all the more. She was able to put aside her heritage, her lineage and her past because she had a need. She put aside her pride to receive the promise of healing. Jesus was impressed by her great faith.

These are four powerful examples of power and persistence in the face of great need. If these women could persist, why can't you? Why do you want to give up the fight? Why are you thinking about quitting? Jesus is standing with His arms open wide—waiting to embrace you and grant your request. Make up your mind to press through the crowd and to touch Him. Demand that you be treated fairly on your job or in your business. You know deep down that through Christ you have the patience of Job, the strength of David, the determination of Esther, and the faith of Abraham. Stand your ground and refuse to be denied.

Don't you know that what God has promised He is also able to provide? Don't you remember that His promises are "yea and amen"? Then you can rest assured that He who promised is faithful. If God said it, He meant it; and His word will not return unto Him void. If you believe that God made you in His image and His likeness, then you also have to believe that you have the same ability to overcome any obstacle, hindrance or challenge in your life. Woman of God, He is on your side!

THE VALUE OF A WOMAN

Many women of God have touched the Master, been delivered and set free, but still act as though they are bound. If you can grab hold of the Word of God, you grab onto the power of God. What the Lord is saying right now is your time has come, but do you realize that you have His anointing on your life? Do you realize how valuable you are to Him?

We must understand the value of a woman. Value is the perceived worth of something or the estimated worth of a person's contributions. Women must also discover their own value and refuse to be treated as anything other than a priceless vessel in the Kingdom of God. If women do not touch Jesus, the Lord will not be free to minister to us. When you discover your value, you call on the virtue of God. You no longer walk with your head down; you walk with your head held high. You no longer walk with your shoulders slumped; you walk straight and tall because you know that your Redeemer lives.

In spite of what men may think or say, if women don't touch God, most of our society will go to hell. If you don't touch God, most of our sons will be in prison. If you don't touch God, most of our men will die prematurely and be buried with their unfulfilled dreams. Keep on touching God. You've got value. Keep on touching God. Don't stop now. Keep on touching God.

If women are not allowed to freely express what God has put in them, our world will be locked up and we will

**Women must also discover their own value
and refuse to be treated as anything other
than a priceless vessel in the Kingdom of God.**

never be free. Woman, the Lord is getting ready to make your hidden talents and gifts so evident that there will be a demand placed on them for the deliverance of

His people. Woman of God, He is going to use you to defile the expectations of men. What man says you cannot do, God is going to do through you because of your faithfulness and because of your commitment. Get ready! God is getting ready to do something spectacular in your life.

THE STRENGTH OF A WOMAN

I have always been amazed at the strength of women to overcome despite the odds. When they are going through trials and tribulations, you may hear them say, "I don't think I can take it anymore," but somehow they find a way to keep going. Some women think their lives are destroyed because a man has left them. They feel like, *I can't make it without him. I'm not sure I can make it by myself. I've never balanced a checkbook and I've never had a job before.* But God will never leave you. Your heavenly Father wants you to know that even if a man abandons you, your life doesn't depend on a man's last name; your life depends on HIS name. You are a child of God and you can overcome every situation in your life through Him.

God wants to use women to save this nation and to share the gospel around the world. Look at churches today. In some instances, you can count the number of men who show up. Many men would rather worship the "television god" than worship the God that their wives and children serve. So it's naïve for us to believe that God will only raise up men and use them for His purpose when they don't spend the time they are supposed to spend with Him. How can God use a man who spends little or no time in prayer? How can God use a man who is not willing to pay the price to sacrifice for the things of God? Why should God only use men to teach when most of them don't have teachable hearts and spirits? It doesn't make natural, spiritual or biblical sense. How can God use a man who is intimidated by a strong, anointed woman to impact the world?

There is one more Scripture I would like to bring to your attention. Do you remember the woman with the very expensive spice who came to anoint Jesus? Matthew 26:6-7 says, "While Jesus was in Bethany in the home of a man known as Simon the Leper, a woman came to him with an alabaster jar of very expensive perfume, which she poured on his head as he was reclining at the table."

This woman had been labeled and was known in her community as "a sinner." Based on the Pharisee's reaction to her, it can be concluded that her occupation was that of a prostitute, so she was not fit to be in the presence of Jesus—much less touch Him. This woman came forward without the permission of the men, thereby breaking protocol according to Jewish custom. Furthermore, this woman came in the presence of the King of kings and did something no one thought should be done. She came with very expensive spice—that she bought with money from her prostitution—and she brought it to Jesus. She did not ask permission. She did not acknowledge the guards or the Pharisees; she just went straight to Jesus. But instead of sending her away, Jesus accepted her gift. Immediately the disciples started to complain:

"Why this waste?" they asked. "This perfume could have been sold at a high price and the money given to the poor." Aware of this, Jesus said to them, "Why are you bothering this woman? She has done a beautiful thing to me. The poor you will always have with you, but you will not always have me. When she poured this perfume on my body, she did it to prepare me for burial. I tell you the truth, wherever this gospel is preached throughout the world, what she has done will also be told, in memory of her" (Matthew 26:8b-13).

The account of this story in the Book of Luke goes into much more detail and shows the depth of love and compassion that Jesus had for this woman—whom society had labeled a sinner:

Now one of the Pharisees invited Jesus to have dinner with him, so he went to the Pharisee's house and reclined at the table. When a woman who had lived a sinful life in that town learned that Jesus was eating at the Pharisee's house, she brought an alabaster jar of perfume, and as she stood behind him at his feet weeping, she began to wet his feet with her tears. Then she wiped them with her hair, kissed them and poured perfume on them. When the Pharisee who had invited him saw this, he said to himself, "If this man were a prophet, he would know who is touching him and what kind of woman she is—that she is a sinner." Jesus answered him, "Simon, I have something to tell you." "Tell me, teacher," he said. "Two men owed money to a certain moneylender. One owed him five hundred denarii, and the other fifty. Neither of them had the money to pay him back, so he canceled the debts of both. Now which of them will love him more?" Simon replied, "I suppose the one who had the bigger debt canceled." "You have judged correctly," Jesus said. Then he turned toward the woman and said to Simon, "Do you see this woman? I came into your house. You did not give me any water for my feet, but she wet my feet with her tears and wiped them with her hair. You did not give me a kiss, but this woman, from the time I entered, has not stopped kissing my feet. You did not put oil on my head, but she has poured perfume on my feet. Therefore, I tell you, her many sins have been forgiven—for she loved much. But he who has been forgiven little loves little." Then Jesus said to her, "Your sins are forgiven." The other guests began to say among themselves, "Who is this who even forgives sins?" Jesus said to the woman, "Your faith has saved you; go in peace" (Luke 7:36-50).

There are so many yokes that we carry around or put ourselves under that prohibit what God wants to do in our lives. God wants us to be free. This woman—a prostitute—did a beautiful thing for Christ. The touch of this woman left such an indelible mark that it will forever be remembered in Scripture.

The Kindness of a Woman

As I reflect over the many years I've ministered and shared the gospel with people, I recall one particular woman who I'm grateful to. This ministry would never have been possible had it not been for a prostitute whose act of faith touched my life. She was living in the Ivory Coast of Western Africa but had AIDS and was about to die. After I led her to the Lord, she came to me and said, "The Lord spoke to me about you. He wants to send you away to go and minister, and He wants me to buy your ticket." She bought me a one-way ticket to France because God was sending me to France as a missionary. The kindness and obedience of a prostitute planted a seed for this international ministry.

From France I moved back to England, and from England I reached the nations of the world. Before coming to America, I planted more than 200 churches in 32 countries—through a prostitute who heard and obeyed the voice of God and bought me a ticket. Never underestimate the value of a woman.

Today I pastor a church of more than 700 families; but when I look back, I remember that whoever I touch through this ministry, I touch them because a prostitute made it possible. Her spirit was the same as that of the prostitute who came to Jesus, preserving the body of Christ by pouring very expensive alabaster oil on Him. It was a wonderful and gracious act—because "how beautiful are the feet of those who bring good news" of Jesus Christ (Rom. 10:15b).

Chapter 4

A Woman's Work
Is Never Done

Sometimes it is hard for men to admit, but it often takes a woman to get something done. Women are diligent and faithful. There is such an anointing from God on the lives of women to get things done, even if it requires hard work, long hours and personal sacrifice. There is an ability and a gift that God has given to women to accomplish things that most men can't (or aren't willing to) do.

**There is an ability and a gift that God has given
to women to accomplish things
that most men can't (or aren't willing to) do.**

And yet I hear so many women say that they feel their work is never done. They spend eight or nine hours each day at the office, then rush home to cook dinner, help the kids with their homework, clean up the house, get the kids to soccer practice and ballet rehearsal, then prepare the children for bed, and finally give their husbands the time and attention they need.

Times have changed. There was a time when the majority of women stayed at home, raised the children and managed the household. Now, because of societal and economic pressures, countless women work full or part-time outside the home and still assume the role of home-maker. Women are still primarily responsible for doing the shopping, preparing meals, rearing the children, cleaning the house, washing the clothes, and the other multitude of tasks that must be completed.

Women who work outside the home and place a high priority on career are often criticized for being selfish and driven. Women who choose to stay at home and avoid the professional workforce are criticized for being lazy or unmotivated. Sometimes it appears that women can't win no matter what they do.

Whether you choose to work inside or outside the home, God has a plan for your life.

A lot of working women—those who are married or have children—feel like they have two full-time jobs, too many demands, too much pressure, and no time for themselves. Trying to skillfully manage both—household and career—has proved to be devastating to the health and sanity of millions of women around the world. As a result, their power and commitment to God begins to dwindle because they are too tired to read the Bible, too tired to pray and fast, too tired to be on fire for God. But whether you choose to work inside or outside the home, God has a plan for your life. He created you with a purpose and a destiny, and He's waiting for you to walk in your calling.

GOD HAS A SPECIFIC PLAN FOR YOUR LIFE

Woman of God, you have not been forsaken; God has not forgotten you. If you have been called to do something for the cause of Christ (and you have), then you can expect to be equipped to fulfill whatever tasks you have been assigned. You have a set time to fulfill the destiny that God has planned for your life, so don't let Scriptures taken out of context put you in the position of having to defend yourself or your calling. When you do something for God, you are going to attract attention, both positive and negative. Just keep your eyes on Jesus and allow Him to lead you. You cannot please everybody because everybody didn't call you; somebody called you, and His name is Jesus.

The Bible says in Romans 11:29 that the gifts and the callings of God are irrevocable, or without repentance. If God has called you, He has already put some gifts in you. If God has called you, He has released some gifts through you. If God has called you, He has placed an anointing on you. God will not change His mind. He knows who you are and what He has called you to do. Do not allow the opinions of others to divert your life.

Think big thoughts and dream big dreams. Do not allow yourself to settle for less than God's best. Don't let society define who you are as a woman. Ask the One who

You cannot please everybody because
everybody didn't call you; somebody
called you, and His name is Jesus.

called you what He called you to do. Yes, there will be challenges, but along with those challenges will be faith and confidence in the Holy Spirit who guides you. Yes, there will be obstacles, but along with those obstacles will be prayer and the ability to persevere. God will give you the answers, the solutions, the grace and the power to move forward and succeed.

A WOMAN OF VALUE AND WORTH

So many women are walking around defeated. The perils of life have weighed them down and discouraged them to the point of despair. There are times when some of you may feel so burdened down by your life that you are tempted to say, "I wish God had created me as a man. Then I would not be facing these difficulties; then my life would be easier."

Others may feel as though they cannot go on always being overlooked, devalued and underappreciated. Yes, you may be tired. And yes, it may be true that you've been overlooked by the world. But know this one thing:

God created you with a purpose in mind, and, woman, your time has come.

Imagine how the Samaritan woman must have felt. She didn't know if anyone could ever see something good in her. Her business was all over town, and everyone had an opinion about her life and judged her. She was being held hostage to her past. She was considered a sinful woman. And in many people's eyes, she was nothing more than a failure—and a disgrace to other women. But when her time came, and she encountered Jesus, her life was changed forever. The Lord wants you to know that the time for you to fulfill your destiny is upon you. Arise! Yes, you have failed before. You are not the first; nor will you be the last person to experience failure. However, in Christ, failure is never final. It is simply a lesson that provides experience and propels you to the next level. Don't give up on God—for He has promised never to leave you or forsake you. In God's eyes, you have value. You are priceless. You are a reflection of His glory, His majesty and His beauty—therefore, you reflect His worth.

Some of you have been told all your life that you are subservient, that you are a servant to your husband. And you've believed all your life that this is the way things are supposed to be. You feel that you're a servant to your husband, a servant to your children and enslaved by your job and daily responsibilities.

Countless women spend their lives waiting for a man to validate them, to make them feel special or important. But that is not what God intended for your life. You are special with or without a man. Single women, take heed. You are better off living alone than being with a man who will break your heart, break your spirit and distract you from the things of God. You are better off being alone than being with a man who doesn't value you the way Jesus values you. You are better off alone than being with someone who diminishes your value and makes you spend your entire life feeling as though you are worthless.

If you have been hurt, or if you have been broken, the time has come for you to bring the broken, shattered pieces of your life to God so He can repair and restore them. God is the Master Potter, and He alone can mend the broken vessel of your life. He alone can wipe your eyes, dry your tears and mend your broken heart. Bring the broken pieces of your life to God and allow Him to put it back together again.

I believe the time has come when God shall cause women to see not only their worth in Him but also begin

God is the Master Potter, and He alone
can mend the broken vessel of your life.

to accept the uniqueness of their womanhood and allow God to do whatever He wants to do in their lives. Thousands of women have sacrificed their own hopes and dreams to promote the hopes and dreams of their boyfriends and husbands. Many of you have put your career aspirations on hold to create doctors and lawyers. You've given up on your own education to advance a man's education. You've worked overtime to support him and helped make him a millionaire. Some of you have made men—whom others considered hopeless and worthless—into successful leaders because of your support and encouragement. And in spite of all the things you have believed and worked for, some of these same men have put you in a place where they make you believe that you are not worth anything. But let me tell you something. In spite of all the things that have been done to you, you can look at them and say, "That is the past, but God has shown me a glorious future."

As a woman, you have value. And anything that has value should be protected. We lock our doors, hide our valuables in safes and vaults, and secure our information with secret passwords. What are you doing to protect

You are a vessel of great worth,

and God wants to protect you.

yourself? Are you fasting and praying to protect yourself from the attacks of the enemy? Are you tithing to protect yourself and your household from being cursed? Are you eating right and exercising to protect your body? Are you following the speed limit laws to protect your safety? Are you reading the Word to protect your mind? You are a vessel of great worth, and God wants to protect you.

God Has Called You to Be a Powerful and Influential Woman

There is a great calling on the lives of women of power and influence. It may be a spiritual call, a call to business, ministry, or marriage and motherhood. There may be a prophetic anointing, healing anointing, preaching anointing or anointing of deliverance in you. I encourage you to ignore the lies of the past and to accept the call of God on your life. Remember that with the call and great anointing is the opportunity and responsibility to minister to God's people and impact the Kingdom.

Proverbs 31 defines a woman of great character. As you read this passage, understand and appreciate who God has called you to be—a powerful and influential woman:

> *A wife of noble character who can find? She is worth far more than rubies. Her husband has full confidence in her and lacks nothing of value. She brings him good, not harm, all the days of her life. She selects wool and flax and works with eager hands. She is like the merchant ships, bringing her food from afar. She gets up while it is still dark; she provides food for her family and portions for her servant girls. She considers a field and buys it; out of her earnings she plants a vineyard. She sets about her work vigorously; her arms are strong for her tasks. She sees that her trading is profitable, and her lamp does not go out at night. In her hand she holds the distaff and grasps the spindle with her fingers. She opens her arms to the*

poor and extends her hands to the needy. When it snows, she has no fear for her household; for all of them are clothed in scarlet. She makes coverings for her bed; she is clothed in fine linen and purple. Her husband is respected at the city gate, where he takes his seat among the elders of the land. She makes linen garments and sells them, and supplies the merchants with sashes. She is clothed with strength and dignity; she can laugh at the days to come. She speaks with wisdom, and faithful instruction is on her tongue. She watches over the affairs of her household and does not eat the bread of idleness. Her children arise and call her blessed; her husband also, and he praises her: "Many women do noble things, but you surpass them all." Charm is deceptive, and beauty is fleeting; but a woman who fears the Lord is to be praised. Give her the reward she has earned, and let her works bring her praise at the city gate.

Woman of power and influence, this is who God created you to be!

CHAPTER 5

DANGEROUS WOMEN AND MEN

Each day there are spiritual traps being set for you—traps designed to ensnare your soul and to destroy your relationship with God. You must be aware of dangerous people because they can literally trap you between life and death, heaven and hell. Learn to trust God completely, for it is He alone who can warn and protect you from the powers of dangerous and wicked people.

Throughout our lifetime we will go through three phases of growth and development in our relationships. It is imperative to nurture and protect these relationships

Learn to trust God completely, for it is He alone
who can warn and protect you from the
powers of dangerous and wicked people.

because they are the very doors that the enemy uses to introduce dangerous people—and dangerous women—into our lives.

STAGES OF RELATIONAL DEVELOPMENT

The first stage is dependency. We are completely dependent on our parents or guardians. We look to them for everything and rely on them to fulfill our hopes, dreams and desires. It is a blessing to have godly parents who train up a child in the way he should go. Because children look to their parents as the first and foremost line of defense, it is tragic when a parent neglects or misleads a child regarding the things of God. What's even more dangerous is when a parent denies or gets in the way of a child giving his or her life to Christ. Jesus gave stern warnings to those who mistreated or hindered His precious little ones.

The second stage of development is independence. That's when we become responsible for our own actions and decisions and accept the consequences for the choices we make. We must be accountable for who we allow into our lives, whose counsel we receive and whose advice we follow. During the stage of independence, it's crucial to surround ourselves with other wise people who can serve as guideposts for our spiritual growth and development.

The third stage is interdependence where there is a mutual exchange of responsibility within our relationships. We're confident in our own abilities as well as of those we've surrounded ourselves with. There is an acknowledgment and appreciation of the fact that "no person is an island," so we rely on and look to each other for support.

It is during this crucial third stage that dangerous people can cause the most damage. Danger commonly arises out of close relationships we've grown to trust and wherein we let down our guard. There are numerous examples in Scripture of dangerous situations and relationships—from the original betrayal in the Garden of Eden to the betrayal of Jesus Christ by one of His own disciples.

DANGEROUS CHARACTERISTICS

There are several examples of dangerous women throughout the Bible. In each circumstance, at least one of three characteristics is easily identifiable: (1) a controlling spirit, (2) a rebellious spirit, and (3) a manipulative spirit.

A *controlling spirit* is rooted in insecurity. Those who feel like they have to control others are insecure with their own power and ability. This is evident in abusive relationships. It seems absurd that a 250-pound man would hit and beat up a 150-pound woman "to keep her in line." His insecurity causes him to lash out at her because he feels the need to control everything she says and everything she does. He is so afraid that she might know more than he knows or might make a better decision than he can, that he does everything to demean and destroy her.

Rebellion is rooted in the spirit of witchcraft. Rebellion is resistance to authority or other types of controls; it is a defiance or opposition to something. Rebellious people are those always creating an uproar and causing discord. Rebellious people are dangerous because they tend to endanger and sacrifice the concerns of others for their own cause. Satan rebelled against God because he wanted to be praised and glorified. He resisted the authority and position of God and tragically influenced one third of the host of heaven into a fallen state.

Manipulation is a perversion of influence. Manipulative people often defraud others and use their power or influence in a negative manner to advance their own cause. In marriage, women can withhold sex and intimacy from their husbands to manipulate a situation to their advantage. In households where the man is the primary breadwinner, husbands can manipulate their wives by withholding or giving money and material things to get their own way. Manipulation is very dangerous because it combines elements of control and rebellion and is often so subtle that it goes undetected.

God did not create us to dominate, control, rebel against or manipulate each other. He created us to coexist and to glorify Him. There must be a mutual respect and appreciation so that these dangerous and negative spirits do not overtake us. The Word clearly tells us there

God did not create us to dominate, control,

rebel against or manipulate each other.

He created us to coexist and to glorify Him.

is nothing new under the sun. As it was in the old days, it still is today. The presence of control, rebellion and manipulation is still very evident in our society.

Disarming Delilah

Let's consider the story of Samson and Delilah found in the Book of Judges. The anointing of God was upon Samson's life to deliver Israel from the Philistines. For years, Samson had been a mighty warrior and exhibited supernatural strength because of the call of God on his life. Samson was raised by God-fearing parents who followed the mandate of the Lord regarding his life. No razor was to be used upon his head to shave his hair, for this was the source of his strength.

Samson met Delilah and fell in love with her. The rulers of Philistine approached Delilah and promised her great reward if she could find out the source of Samson's strength and deliver him into their hands.

Three times Samson misled Delilah regarding the source of his strength. Finally, after much prodding, he revealed his secret. "No razor has ever been used on my head," he said, "because I have been a Nazirite set apart to God since birth. If my head were shaved, my strength would leave me, and I would become as weak as any other man" (Judges 16:17).

What's interesting about this is how Delilah manipulated Samson for money, saying things like, "How can you say you love me and not tell me the secret of your strength?" She pressed the issue until he finally gave in. After the Philistines seized Samson and gouged out his eyes, there is no further mention of Delilah. This dangerous woman used manipulation and seduction to get what she wanted, and then she was gone.

Samson's parents did their best to protect him—and his gift from God—and raise him according to God's law because they knew he had been set apart to do a mighty work. But once Samson reached the stage of interdependence where he placed a high value on other external relationships, there was not a lot his parents could do to protect him.

Delilah was an attractive but dangerous woman because she used her beauty and sexual prowess to manipulate and disarm Samson. From the very beginning, her intentions were to do him harm and to deliver him into the hands of the Philistine army. She was calculating, methodical and manipulative. And because of his lust and weakness for dangerous women, Samson fell prey to her trap.

No Other Like Jezebel

When it comes to dangerous women, possibly no other woman has been so notoriously named for being controlling, rebellious and manipulative as Jezebel. The very name of Jezebel is still used as a general description for a wicked and spiteful woman.

Every Woman in the Bible provides clear insight into the life of Jezebel, her disdain for the God of Israel, and the adversarial relationship between her and her husband, King Ahab:

> Jezebel was the daughter of the kind of Sidon, and was totally committed to the virulent form of Baal worship practiced there. Her marriage to Ahab resulted in Ahab worshiping the Sidonian deity and cooperating with

Jezebel in her efforts to make Baal the god of Israel. She came close to succeeding.

First Kings 18:4 and 13 make it clear that Jezebel took the initiative in this religious crusade, for the text tells us that "Jezebel killed the prophets of the Lord." This does not mean that she personally killed God's prophets, but rather that they were killed at her command. This and other references to Jezebel in the Old Testament make it clear that she was a forceful woman. In many ways Jezebel dominated her husband and set the course of the kingdom. God responded to the threat posed by Jezebel by raising up the prophet Elijah. Elijah not only turned the hearts of the people back to the Lord, but he predicted Jezebel's death as a punishment from God.

Jezebel was a determined opponent of God, set on wiping out His prophets and purging Israel of worshipers of the Lord. She initiated a campaign to exterminate God's prophets and threatened Elijah's life.

Jezebel exercised dominance over her royal husband. This is particularly striking because Ahab was a skilled military man and capable ruler....Yet the biblical text suggests that his wife, Jezebel, dominated Ahab.[1]

THE WITCH OF EN DOR

Finally, one of the lesser known dangerous women of the Bible has come to be known as the witch of En Dor. In actuality, she was not a true witch, but rather a medium through which she channeled ungodly spirits. She was being controlled and manipulated by demonic forces. This dangerous woman can be found in the Book of First Samuel.

During the conquest, En Dor was a Canaanite stronghold that the Israelites had not been able to possess (Josh. 17:11). The city did lie in Israelite-controlled territory, however, and Saul, in obedience to Deuteronomy 18's condemnation of occult practices of every kind, had set out to exterminate all mediums and spiritists (1 Sam. 28:9).

However, when the Philistines invaded Israel, and every attempt of Saul to seek counsel from the Lord was refused, the desperate king demanded that his servants find him a medium. When one was located at En Dor, Saul went there in disguise to consult with the demon that was her spirit contact.

Like others dedicated to the occult, this woman had linked her future to evil forces. Despite the campaign Saul had launched to exterminate such persons, the medium of En Dor had been unable to break the spiritual bonds that held her. She lived in fear of exposure, yet was addicted to the relationship that had been established. What a tragic life this medium must have lived, knowing that her spiritual addiction was wrong, fearful that her secret might be discovered, and yet unwilling or unable to rid herself of the demonic.

The Old Testament teaches the reality of demonic beings that seek to influence and harm human beings. These demons are actually fallen angels who followed Satan in his great prehistoric rebellion against God. While some so-called occult practices are mere trickery, true occult practices do tap into the supernatural and serve as avenues through which demons can contact and influence human beings. For this reason the Bible condemns every occult practice, from the reading of horoscopes to the spiritist's and medium's actual contact with demons. According to Old Testament Law, anyone who engaged in any such practice in Israel was to be executed.[2]

A World Full of Danger

The spirits of Delilah and Jezebel are still alive and well today. Controlling, rebellious and manipulative spirits are evident as men and women are caught in the grips of blackmail, fraud, crime and violence. Greed, the desire for power, illicit sexual freedom and an overall decline in morality are creating even more opportunities for sin to destroy lives.

The newspaper headlines are filled with stories about corporate scandals, adulterous love affairs and reliance on horoscopes and astrology to predict the future. Television commercials are inundated with messages about the occult; they advertise psychic mediums, 900-number hotlines and tarot cards to predict the future. All these things are an abhorrence to God.

Even today, the world is filled with controlling, rebellious, manipulative—dangerous—women; those who lie, cheat and steal to get their way. Just as there are dangerous women, there are also dangerous men. As believers in Jesus Christ and children of God, we must be careful with whom we develop relationships and allow to get close to us. Even so, it's comforting to know that nothing—not even dangerous people—can separate us from the love of Christ.

ENDNOTES

1. Sue and Larry Richards, *Every Woman in the Bible* (Nashville, TN: Thomas Nelson, 1999), 138-139.

2. Ibid, 125-126.

CHAPTER 6

HINDRANCES TO A
WOMAN'S INFLUENCE

Everyone in the world wants to experience love. Women, in particular, know that love is the greatest force and the greatest gift that can be offered. We know that it is important for us to stay close to God for God is LOVE. We don't want to be separated from God or for Him to be disappointed in us. Whosoever loves is born of God and knows God.

The term "love for God" indicates reverence or the fear of the Lord. Fear of the Lord does not refer to the "terror" type of fear; it means you reverence God to the point that you love God and want to serve Him. Love is the essential element in life. We want God to love us. We do things for Him because we desire that love and because we love Him.

Just as the psalmist David wanted to please the Lord, we also want to please God because He is the source of our lives. This is the same attitude we are to reflect in our relationships. Consider these three profound verses of Psalm 133:

How good and pleasant it is when brothers live together in unity! It is like precious oil poured on the head, running down on the beard, running down on Aaron's beard, down upon the collar of his robes. It is as if the dew of Hermon were falling on Mount Zion. For there the Lord bestows his blessing, even life forevermore (Psalm 133:1-3).

There is a blessing that comes from God when His children live together in unity and in love. God uses people to take care of one another; therefore, unity is something that we all need to strive for in our lives.

We want God to love us. We do things
for Him because we desire that love
and because we love Him.

Imagine when we decide as a unit to do something for God—there is nothing that we won't be able to accomplish. The devil knows that. One of the ways and the tricks that the devil uses to destroy unity is to bring *disunity*. If there is disunity in the lives of women (as well as men), their influence will be greatly hindered, diminishing the power in their daily lives to impact the world as God intended. There is a way to maintain a relationship with God as well as a way to destroy a relationship with God. There is a way to maintain a relationship with people and a way to destroy relationships with people.

One of the things that we have to keep in mind is this: If we are going to walk in unity and impact our world, there are twelve pitfalls we must avoid, lest we hinder the blessings of God in our lives and in the Church.

STRIFE

It is to a man's honor to avoid strife, but every fool is quick to quarrel (Proverbs 20:3).

The first pitfall that will directly hinder the influence of women is strife. The word *strife* means to oppose or become an adversary. An adversary is one who verbally disputes or argues; one who nags; or one who condescends. A woman who is involved in strife will render her influence in her home, at her job, and in her relationships with others ineffective. She will be unable to perform and do the things that God intended for her to do.

The sister of strife is anger. Anger can destroy your life. The Bible says that a person who is easily angered is a fool. "A fool gives full vent to his anger, but a wise man keeps himself under control" (Prov. 29:11). Although God says you can be angry at times, He also says that we should not let the sun go down on our anger (Eph. 4:26).

If you carry strife with you as you get older, you will give yourself over to a premature death. Heart attacks, high blood pressure, nerve conditions, and anxiety rest in the bosom of a person who promotes strife and is quarrelsome. We all exhibit temper in differing degrees. Even babies display temper. If you don't change their diapers regularly or feed them when they are hungry, they will display their temper.

However, there are adult women who still throw childish temper tantrums. They use their anger as a crutch in an attempt to manipulate and get their own

If you carry strife with you as you get older,
you will give yourself over to a premature death.

way, causing much harm. Marriages, families and friendships are destroyed because of strife. Businesses and churches are destroyed because of strife. Entire lives are destroyed because of anger and strife. If you are a person who lives in strife, you will destroy the blessings in your life and cut off the ability to influence people with your gifts. Are you a person of strife? If so, you need to acknowledge it and deal with it before you can truly be productive in your relationships and in your work.

ENVY

Anger is cruel and fury overwhelming, but who can stand before jealousy? (Proverbs 27:4)

The words *envy* and *jealousy* carry with them a hot temper; a hostile, disruptive spirit; a spirit that wants to destroy things, that wants to disrupt the calm of unity, that wants to stop the flow of peace. A spouse with a jealous spirit or a spirit of envy can cause division or disruption within the home and cause that home to become a place of hostile activity. A good example of this is in the Book of Genesis: "When Rachel saw that she was not bearing Jacob any children, she became jealous of her sister. So she said to Jacob, 'Give me children, or I'll die!' " (Gen. 30:1) Rachel showed her hostility, her envy and her jealousy of her older sister Leah. Leah had been able to give children to her husband when Rachel was not able to do the same. Her envy certainly had a disruptive effect on their relationship, as envy will have on your relationships.

BEARING GRUDGES

Do not make friends with a hot-tempered man, do not associate with one easily angered, or you may learn his ways and get yourself ensnared (Proverbs 22:24-25).

When Paul wrote to the Corinthian church, he told them that love, which truly makes a woman's influence powerful, would not keep a record of wrongs. Love doesn't harbor negative events and feelings from the past. Love does not have a notebook listing everything that a husband, child, coworker, or boss has done. Love freely releases other people and extends mercy. A woman who bears a grudge will not be effective as a witness or as an influence in her sphere of activity.

Love doesn't harbor negative
events and feelings from the past.

The Scripture at the beginning of this section gives a warning: Don't even make friends with hot-tempered men or women. Do not associate with someone who gets angry easily. If you do so, you will also become trapped in their ways. So many people who bear grudges do so simply because they hang around other people who bear grudges. If you are married to someone who always carries grudges, it won't take long before you begin to take on their spirit.

UNTEACHABLE SPIRIT

Since an overseer is entrusted with God's work, he must be blameless–not overbearing, not quick-tempered, not given to drunkenness, not violent, not pursuing dishonest gain (Titus 1:7).

One of the purposes of women in the Church, particularly older women of a church, is to teach the younger women. However, a woman will not be able to teach effectively unless she first is teachable. Women in the Church need to develop a teachable spirit so they will be able to teach. A woman who is unteachable will never be able to develop to properly teach the women in their church as was intended by the apostle Paul when he wrote to both young pastors, Timothy and Titus.

In addition, teaching must not come from those who have done things wrong or those who have messed up their lives, but from women in the Church who can testify to the correctness of their actions as well as the corrections of their mistakes. In this way the power of negative behavior is diminished as the emphasis of teaching is placed not on negativity but on the positive.

Some people don't want you to teach them anything. They cooperate only if they can get their way. If you have an unteachable spirit, it will be difficult for the Holy Spirit to walk with you. The Holy Spirit is a teacher and He only teaches those who yield to Him. You can distinguish those people who have the Holy Spirit in their lives from

A woman will not be able to teach effectively unless she first is teachable.

those who simply have head knowledge and want to teach. The latter group have not attainted to the status of "older women" who are qualified to teach. They are as children who themselves need to be taught.

There are some who want their own selfish power to be felt. They are overbearing and like to exert a dangerous controlling power. They try to affect people's lives in detrimental ways instead of building them up.

The King James Version of the Bible says,

For a bishop must be blameless, as the steward of God; not self-willed, not soon angry, not given to wine, no striker, not given to filthy lucre; but a lover of hospitality, a lover of good men, sober, just, holy, temperate; holding fast the faithful word as he hath been taught, that he may be able by sound doctrine both to exhort and to convince the gainsayers. For there are many unruly and vain talkers and deceivers, specially they of the circumcisions: whose mouths must be stopped, who subvert whole houses, teaching things which they ought not, for filthy lucre's sake (Titus 1:7-11).

If you have an unteachable spirit, you will hinder your own blessings and directly affect the influence you are able to extend in life.

SELFISHNESS

> *Love is patient, love is kind. It does not envy, it does not boast, it is not proud. It is not rude, it is not self-seeking, it is not easily angered, it keeps no record of wrongs* (1 Corinthians 13:4-5).

If you are selfish, it will affect every aspect of your life. You will hinder friendship with God and your relationships with others.

For a woman to be effective, she must not always consider what's in it for her. The Lord Jesus Christ even said, "The Son of Man came not to be ministered unto, but to minister, and to give his life a ransom for many" (Mt. 20:28 KJV). A woman who will not serve, who will not give up willingly and unselfishly to serve other people, will be rendered ineffective by a spirit that is wrapped up in herself.

It is important that whatever you do, you teach others to do the same so that when you are not there, they will be able to carry on what you are doing. Don't be selfish by thinking you are the only person who can do the job. This type of attitude will not advance your cause but will rather hinder it. You must rid yourself of selfishness before you can influence others for good.

Insecurity

[Love] *is not rude, it is not self-seeking, it is not easily angered, it keeps no record of wrongs. Love does not delight in evil but rejoices with the truth. It always protects, always trusts, always hopes, always perseveres* (1 Corinthians 13:5-7).

A woman who is not secure in who she is, in the giftings that God has given her, in her relationship to her family or in her relationship to her friends, cannot be effective in influencing anyone in this world.

There are some women who are very insecure and subsequently they find themselves doing unnecessary things. Some of you see your husband talking to somebody and suddenly your heart begins to faint and anger takes over. You get in the car to go home and won't speak to anyone because you assume somebody wants to have an affair with your spouse.

An insecure person in leadership can cause a lot of trouble because they become territorial and controlling.

Some of you became insecure when you were a child because your father left home unexpectedly with no explanation of his extended absence. You may have become insecure because you lost your husband or wife to another person, or because you lost your job. Now, as a result of your internal insecurity, you try to control everything around you.

If you have acted in this manner, you don't need to feel guilty; but, instead, you need to deal with the insecurity in your life so that you can have a positive influence in your world. Get rid of the guilt and deal with the insecurity so that you can move forward and have peace in your life.

HIDDEN AGENDAS

Finally...whatever is true, whatever is noble, whatever is right, whatever is pure, whatever is lovely, whatever is admirable—if anything is excellent or praiseworthy— think about such things (Philippians 4:8).

A woman must make sure that the motives for everything that she does are clear, open and honest before God and man. We must not allow ourselves to be deceived into thinking that we are doing something good

Whatever you do,

do it from a pure heart.

for somebody else when, at the heart of the matter, we have our own interest as the priority.

If you have a hidden agenda, get rid of it. Whatever you do, do it from a pure heart. Your motives in leading others will become apparent—even if unstated—and the cooperation you receive from others may be directly related to whether or not you have a hidden agenda as the motive which drives your actions.

EGO

To fear the Lord is to hate evil; I hate pride and arrogance, evil behavior and perverse speech (Proverbs 8:13).

The word *ego* is another word for pride. The word *pride* literally means to rise up. Proverbs 16:18a says, "Pride goes before destruction." A person who is headed toward destruction cannot be a positive influence to the people around them. A woman who allows her ego or pride to rise up within her will cause her life to be ineffective in contributing to positive change in others.

Pride in itself is not wrong. *The pride that is destructive is pride in our self rather than pride in the God who gives us the ability to be effective.* A woman of God must learn to have pride in the God who created her in His image, walk in the image of God, and allow the image of God to rise up within her; not exalt the image of her own fallen nature, which will destroy her influence.

People with large egos never accomplish much of anything, least of all effect a positive influence on others. From time to time we get carried away with ego—like a peacock—strutting our stuff. Come to recognize that you can accomplish much more by putting ego aside and learning to work as a team and to lead with a team goal in mind!

SUSPICION

Fear of man will prove to be a snare but whoever trusts in the Lord is kept safe (Proverbs 29:25).

Suspicion can destroy relationships with God as well as with those around you. Sometimes in the Church and in business we have women (and men) who claim they have the gift of discernment when what they have is simply a nature of suspicion. A suspicious person is a person who lives in fear and consequently looks for things to fall apart around them; they look for things to happen to cause the desires of their heart to fail.

A woman of influence cannot allow suspicion to inhabit her thoughts because that suspicion will destroy her ability to think rationally, to act rationally, and to act as a person of influence. Sadly, persons who are suspicious live looking over their shoulder, as though people are after them to hurt them or destroy them. A woman of influence, however, believes that the God who called her is the God who is able to sustain, to keep and to protect because she dwells in the secret place and abides under the shadow of the Almighty. She is confident of God's abiding protection which enables her to function as a woman of influence.

UNFORGIVENESS

Therefore I tell you, whatever you ask for in prayer, believe that you have received it, and it will be yours. And when you stand praying, if you hold anything against anyone, forgive him, so that your Father in heaven may forgive you your sins (Mark 11:24-26).

Jesus had a lot to say about the spirit of unforgiveness and how it can render one's life ineffective. He taught us to pray: "Forgive us our debts as we forgive our debtors." Another translation says, "Forgive us our trespasses as we forgive those who trespass against us."

When we refuse to forgive others, the forgiveness of God cannot flow properly into our own lives. When the forgiveness of God does not flow properly in our lives, then we cannot be an effective influence on others

We all have differences among us from time to time because we all have imperfections and sharp edges; it is only through the grace and mercy of God that we are able to walk through our failures. But if we are not able to receive the grace and the mercy of God extended to us because we have not extended grace and mercy to those who have failed us, we will never be what God intended for us to be. Nor will we have the capability to succeed in being a positive influence or blessing to others.

When we refuse to forgive others,

the forgiveness of God cannot flow

properly into our own lives.

If you have unforgiveness in your heart, it will affect you. It will negatively impact your relationships—with God, with one another, at church and on your job—and it will certainly diminish your sphere of influence.

SPIRIT OF SLANDER

A perverse man stirs up dissension, and a gossip separates close friends (Proverbs 16:28).

The word *slander* is an unusual word. A slanderer is one who gossips; one who defames; one who gives an evil report; one who whispers.

Whenever one woman says to another, "Come here and let me whisper in your ear what I just heard," slander is transported. A slanderer is someone who whispers; it is someone who gives an evil report about another individual. She is a talebearer as described in the King James Version—someone who tells an unbecoming story about another individual and spreads it rather than releasing a covering for that sin. Proverbs 17:9 says, "He who covers over an offense promotes love, but whoever repeats the matter separates close friends."

The Bible also says love covers a multitude of sins but a slanderer is one who brings out a multitude of sins. Slandering is a means of destruction. It is not a means of building up, and people who destroy other people with words that they speak will never be able to build up and influence the lives of people with whom they come in contact.

Slander and gossip are dangerous. You need to make certain these traits don't work in your life, or your potential influence will be stopped dead in its tracks.

LACK OF TRUST

He will have no fear of bad news; his heart is stead-fast, trusting in the Lord (Psalm 112:7).

All effective and influential individuals must learn to trust. First of all their trust must be in God and their relationships must be intact—not subject to any of the eleven other hindrances we have outlined. It is when a relationship is not intact that the things mentioned in this particular chapter will cause a woman's influence to be rendered ineffective.

Secondly, a woman must trust her husband and her family. She must trust her friends and her coworkers. Lack of trust will cause the inability to establish effective and positive relationships with other people. Sometimes our trust will be betrayed, as in Psalm 41:9, when the psalmist says, "Even my close friend, whom I trusted, he who shared my bread, has lifted up his heel against me." When your trust is betrayed, you cannot allow yourself not to trust again; you must continue to trust.

Sometimes people will feel that even God has failed them. When you feel like that, you still have to step out and say, "God, I trust You. I don't care what happens to me; I don't care what circumstances come in this life; I am going to be a person of trust." Job said, "Though he slay me, yet will I hope in him" (Job 13:15a).

If you don't trust anyone, no one will trust you. You have to trust. If you trust people, then you will often see a great reward in their reciprocal trust and respect for you. A woman of influence must be a woman who trusts. Trust is a positive influence in her world.

CHAPTER 7

A CONQUERING SPIRIT

Jesus left that place and went to the vicinity of Tyre. He entered a house and did not want anyone to know it; yet he could not keep his presence secret. In fact, as soon as she heard about him, a woman whose little daughter was possessed by an evil spirit came and fell at his feet. The woman was a Greek, born in Syrian Phoenicia. She begged Jesus to drive the demon out of her daughter. "First let the children eat all they want," he told her, "for it is not right to take the children's bread and toss it to their dogs." "Yes, Lord," she replied, "but even the dogs under the table eat the children's crumbs." Then he told her, "For such a reply, you may go; the demon has left your daughter." She went home and found her child lying on the bed, and the demon gone (Mark 7:24-30).

Who was this woman who was determined enough even to interrupt the plans of Jesus? She was a desperate woman with a need, a woman who would go to any length to meet that need, a woman with a conquering spirit.

Jesus had wanted to keep His whereabouts a secret; yet, somehow this lady persisted until she found where He was staying and did not hesitate to plead for help. The fact that she was Greek and Jesus was a Jew did not stop her either. She had been carrying a great burden at home and was laden with a situation that overwhelmed her—her daughter was possessed by an evil spirit. She decided that whatever she needed to do, she would do. She needed a miracle and was determined to find the One who could give her that miracle.

The Bible tells us that as soon as she heard about Him, she came and fell at His feet. She begged Jesus to drive the demon out of the daughter. She said, "My daughter is possessed and I need somebody to conquer this spirit."

She needed a miracle and was determined to find the One who could give her that miracle.

There was such a tenacity in her spirit that she would not give up. Even when Jesus tried to discourage her by saying, "First let the children eat all they want for it is not right to take the children's bread and toss it to their dogs," she replied that even the dogs under the table eat the children's crumbs. She was determined to receive what she needed.

Jesus was impressed with her reply. She hadn't come to be discouraged nor was she willing to go away empty-handed. She came with a conquering spirit to receive victory. And the Bible says that the woman went her way believing. Although she had never met or spoken to Jesus before, she demonstrated faith. When she went away, she had conquered her problem. This woman had a *conquering spirit.*

THE FAITH OF A CONQUERING SPIRIT

What is it in women that actually gives them the strength to conquer any problem or situation? It's called faith. Every woman who believes in Jesus possesses it. Faith overcomes the world.

> *Now faith is being sure of what we hope for and certain of what we do not see. This is what the ancients were commended for. By faith we understand that the universe was formed at God's command, so that what is seen was not made out of what was visible* (Hebrews 11:1-3).

Women possess a conquering spirit to such an extent that they even ask for the impossible.

In Hebrews 11 we find a list of patriarchs of the faith—Abraham, Abel, Enoch, Noah, Jacob, Joseph, Moses, and on and on. Then we come to verse 31 and there we find listed the name of a prostitute, Rahab, whom most of us would consider an outcast, but she, by faith, came to be numbered among those who conquered. Then also consider verse 35 very carefully: "Women received back their dead, raised to life again." Women possess a conquering spirit to such an extent that they even ask for the impossible.

CONQUERING DEATH AND SORROW

Martha, the sister of Mary and Lazarus, was another woman with a conquering spirit. According to John chapter 11, after Lazarus had been dead for four days, Jesus finally arrived in Bethany at the home of Mary and Martha. Martha met Jesus outside their home and said to Him, "Lord, if you had been here, my brother would not have died. But I know that even now God will give you whatever you ask" (Jn. 11:21-22).

Martha had not given up. She indicated to Jesus that even when everything looked hopeless, she still had faith that God would give Jesus whatever He asked. In the end, she was able to conquer both sorrow and death.

Every Woman Can Have a Conquering Spirit

Whenever you find a woman who has developed a conquering spirit, that woman will not rest until her passion, until her drive, until her motivation meets its answer!

In spite of a woman's potential for timidity, there is a conquering spirit deep within that says you can dream big and realize those dreams. How many years have women been told they can never be leaders or preachers or successful businesspeople? Yet, they have proven time and time again that in spite of the odds, women can conquer and their works will show forth.

Conquerors are not born; they are made. They are made through the circumstances, challenges, and difficulties of life. You can't conquer anything until first you are faced with a problem that you are able to defeat. Conquerors are those people who are not intimidated by a mountain. They walk toward it and climb one step at a time because that is the only way they can get to the top.

Women must stand up and decide to conquer their insecurities, their fears, and their low self-esteem. When a woman decides she can conquer those things that the enemy uses to trap and deceive and make her feel worthless, she will overcome sickness and disease, mental and

Conquerors are not born; they are made.

emotional breakdown, financial and family difficulties. She will see herself as a woman who has emerged out of her challenges and struggles victorious. No matter what she has been through that was meant to destroy her, God will show forth His goodness in her. What the enemy meant for evil, God will turn around for good. A victorious woman determines to overcome the negative things and commits to battling the deficiencies in her life. She decides to fight laziness, strife, division, jealousy, slander—all those things that will prevent her from succeeding in life. Petty things do not destroy the great plan of God in her life. She decides to move on with God, not allow little annoying obstacles to slow her progress or divert her attention from the goal—a higher calling. There is a conquering spirit within you!

Today, stand up in Jesus' name to overcome that negative feeling. Your gender, your weakness, your defects may point at you, but there is something inside you that is pointing back and that is your faith in God. Today as a woman with a conquering spirit, you can say: "...greater is he that is in me than he that is in the world" (1 Jn. 4:4 KJV).

You may be down, but you are not out. You may be left to die, but God is waiting to resurrect you. You may be written off but God is about to assign you. The great days of your life are yet ahead. No matter what the enemy has done, you are about to see what God will do. The days of victory are ahead!

CHARACTERISTICS OF A CONQUERING WOMAN

Challenge yourself to be a conquering woman and determine to build the following traits in your life as a victorious woman of God:

1. A conquering woman is dominated by the Word of God. God's Word is the guiding force in her life.
2. A conquering woman maintains a positive thought life. As a woman thinks in her heart, so is she. If she thinks she is a failure, she will be setting herself up to fail. If she thinks she is a loser, she may just be preparing herself to lose. However, when she begins to see herself with the eyes of God, she will journey down a road of success.
3. Conquerors have the ability to create their own reality. They don't make a bed of defeat, but one of victory. They determine not to drink from the cup of shame, but out of the cup of victory. They have the ability to create their own reality.
4. Conquerors realize a beneficial lesson in every challenge or adversity they face. They decide that every situation is an opportunity for God to show His power. Age, marital status, race, or

physical condition is not a factor to them. They know they can conquer because the One who is in them is greater than their surroundings.

As a woman thinks in her heart, so is she.

5. Conquering women are winners who were past losers determined not to quit. Most successful people have failed on their road to success. It is the conquering spirit within and the "can do" attitude that propels successful women past their less determined sisters.

6. Conquering women excel in the areas of their choice. They excel in God; excel in marriage; excel on the job; excel in vision; excel in their call. Whatever God has placed in them, they are determined to excel.

Conquering women are winners
who were past losers determined not to quit.

7. Conquerors consider their limitations to be temporary. "The sky is the limit." When two or more conquering women are in agreement, they accomplish amazing things and can turn the world upside down.

8. A conquering woman is successful because she is committed to a cause.

9. A conqueror is one who knows the need for support, cooperation and partnership. Conquering women are not intimidated to ask for help. They know two heads are better than one and focus on the victory and not who brought it about.

10. Conquering women possess a great level of discernment and use it for the glory of God.

It is important that women of destiny take their place in the Kingdom in preparation "for such a time as this." Those gifts that you've abandoned because of criticism, go back today and reclaim them. Those talents that you have left aside because of what people have thought about you, choose today to develop them. Those people who would stand in your way and try to keep you from the course God has shown for you, bind them today and move forward.

Women, you were born for greatness. God wants to use you to accomplish mighty things, and He has equipped you for it. You are called to be a dedicated wife, a loving mother, a comforting sister, a wise grandmother, a committed Christian, a responsible coworker. Your achievements in life will have positive influence. If there are gifts that have laid dormant in you, provoke them to come forth. As a conquering woman, you can come against the spirit of fear. You can come against the spirit of condemnation and against the spirit of shame. You can take your place as a woman of power, a woman of strength, and a woman who has conquered every opposition the enemy has targeted against you.

CHAPTER 8

WOMEN WHO
CHANGED THE WORLD

If you are a woman in ministry, or a woman with the call of God on your life, then you have a vision and a destiny that you must fulfill. There is something that God has put within you to do, and it is your responsibility to discover your calling, fulfill your destiny and change your world.

Kathryn Kuhlman was a woman who changed the world. Although not a lot was known about her—and the world didn't know her by name—she was by far one of the

It is your responsibility to discover your calling,

fulfill your destiny and change your world.

most powerful and anointed women in ministry who has ever graced the pulpit. Her ministry touched the lives of men and women all around the globe. Her legendary healing ministry and undeniable reliance on the gifts and power of the Holy Spirit is still impacting the generations.

One of the leading evangelists in the world, Benny Hinn, frequently says that Kathryn Kuhlman's ministry changed his life and prepared him for the powerful ministry of teaching and healing he leads today.

In her book, *I Believe in Miracles,* Kathryn Kuhlman wrote:

A little knowledge and an overabundance of zeal always tends to be harmful. In the area involving religious truths, it can be disastrous.

God the Father planned and purposed the creation and the redemption of man, and is in our vernacular, the Big Boss. God the Son provided and purchased at Calvary what the Father had planned in eternity. He made possible the realization of God's eternal plan. All that we receive from the Father *must* come through Jesus Christ the Son, and that is why at the heart of our faith is a Person—the very Son of the very God. When we pray, we come before the Father's Throne in Jesus' Name. We cannot obtain an audience with the Father, except we come to Him in the Name of His Son.

But the Holy Spirit is the *power* of the Trinity. It was *His* power which raised Jesus from the dead. It is that *same* Resurrection power that flows through our physical bodies today, healing and sanctifying.

In short, when we pray in the Name of Jesus, the Father looks down through the complete perfection, the utter holiness, the absolute righteousness of His only Begotten Son, knowing that by Him, the price was paid in full for man's redemption, and in Him, lies the answer to every human need.

God honors the redemptive work of His Son by giving to us through Him, the desires of our hearts. Thus, while it is the Resurrection power of the Holy Spirit which performs the actual healing of the physical body, Jesus made it perfectly clear that we are to look to Him, the Son, in faith, for He is the One who has made all these things possible.[1]

These poignant words are indicative of the power and influence that flowed through this mighty woman of God who changed the world. Kathryn knew she was called to be a powerful and influential woman in spite of what men, tradition and society dictated. She saw herself the way God saw her—and allowed herself to be used for His purposes. This anointed woman of God didn't allow the apparent limitations of her gender to keep her from pursuing her destiny. She kept her eyes on Jesus rather than looking at the waves and winds of tradition. In the midst of a male-dominated religious order, she stepped out on faith into her calling and changed the world.

It is time to destroy some lies and myths that the world has created about women. It is time to restore the dreams that women have had and help them return to the optimism of their youth. Remember the childlike faith you had as a little girl—the faith that said you could do anything and be anything you wanted to be? God wants you to pick it back up again and renew your faith in Him. He wants you to start pursuing the vision that He has put in your heart again. He wants you to rediscover the hopes and dreams you've lost along the way; He wants you to recover the lost opportunities that passed you by and the goals that seemed impossible.

ONE WOMAN CHANGED THE ENTIRE WORLD

From the beginning of time, women have had the power to change the world. It requires faith, commitment and obedience to God's Word to yield that power for good. Unfortunately, in Genesis chapter 3, a different kind of monumental history was made:

> *Now the serpent was more crafty than any of the wild animals the Lord God had made. He said to the woman, "Did God really say, 'You must not eat from any tree in the garden'?" The woman said to the serpent, "We may eat fruit from the trees in the garden, but God did say, 'You must not eat fruit from the tree that is in the middle of the garden, and you must not touch it, or you will die.' " "You will not surely die," the serpent said to the woman. "For God knows that when you eat of it your eyes will be opened, and you will be like God, knowing good and evil."*
>
> *When the woman saw that the fruit of the tree was good for food and pleasing to the eye, and also desirable for gaining wisdom, she took some and ate it. She also gave some to her husband, who was with her, and he ate it. Then the eyes of both of them were opened, and they realized they were naked; so they sewed fig leaves together and made coverings for themselves.*
>
> *Then the man and his wife heard the sound of the Lord God as he was walking in the garden in the cool of the day, and they hid from the Lord God among the trees of the garden. But the Lord God called to the man, "Where are you?" He answered, "I heard you in the garden, and I was afraid because I was naked; so*

I hid." And he said, "Who told you that you were naked? Have you eaten from the tree that I commanded you not to eat from?" The man said, "The woman you put here with me—she gave me some fruit from the tree, and I ate it."

Then the Lord God said to the woman, "What is this you have done?" The woman said, "The serpent deceived me, and I ate."...To the woman he said, "I will greatly increase your pains in childbearing; with pain you will give birth to children. Your desire will be for your husband, and he will rule over you."

To Adam he said, "Because you listened to your wife and ate from the tree about which I commanded you, 'You must not eat of it,' cursed is the ground because of you; through painful toil you will eat of it all the days of your life. It will produce thorns and thistles for you, and you will eat the plants of the field. By the sweat of your brow you will eat your food until you return to the ground, since from it you were taken; for dust you are and to dust you will return" (Genesis 3:1-13,16-19).

One woman—Eve—literally changed the world. When God asked Eve, "What is this you have done?" she could have answered, "Lord, I have just changed the world." Through the act of one woman, the entire course of history was altered.

God pronounced curses on the serpent, on women and on mankind. He banished Adam and Eve from the garden and intensified the work that was required for sustenance and to bring forth children. Life as they knew it in the Garden of Eden would never be the same.

But just as the enemy used one woman to throw off the entire world order, God also used one woman to set it back on course. Through one woman He brought forth the redemptive Person of Jesus Christ, who would break the curses, bruise the head of the serpent and restore the fallen state of humanity.

God used one woman—Mary, mother of Jesus—to birth grace, mercy and salvation into the earth. Mary, a humble and righteous woman had found favor with God: "Mary, you have found favor with God. You will be with child and give birth to a son, and you are to give him the name Jesus. He will be great and will be called the Son of

Just as the enemy used one woman to throw off the entire world order, God also used one woman to set it back on course.

the Most High. The Lord God will give him the throne of his father David, and he will reign over the house of Jacob forever; his kingdom will never end" (Lk. 1:30b-33).

There are women of the Bible who have gone down in history because of their commitment and dedication to God and family. And there are women all around the world who have sacrificed everything because of their love for their country, their family, their God and their beliefs. They have left a permanent mark in the annals of history that no one can erase. They have realized the value and contributions of their womanhood.

OTHER WOMEN OF POWER AND INFLUENCE

Following are several brief profiles of women who changed the world during a time when the character, credibility and contributions of women were still being questioned.

Susan B. Anthony paired with Elizabeth Cady Stanton to form one of the most influential teams in American history. Anthony grew up in a Quaker family and began her life of social reform by speaking out against drunkenness and slavery. Recruited by Stanton, her emphasis changed to women's rights and eventually she focused solely on passage of a Constitutional Amendment giving women the right to vote. Anthony remained single during her life, which freed her up to travel widely and work to mobilize people on behalf of the movement. In 1869, Stanton and Anthony founded the National Women Suffrage Association and together they published a weekly newspaper that set forth their radical ideas.

Amelia Earhart was born in Atchison, Kansas, in 1897. In her early twenties, she became fascinated with aviation. Earhart was the first woman pilot to make a solo flight across the Atlantic in 1932, duplicating the feat which had made Charles Lindbergh famous just five years earlier. (She was also the first woman to fly across the Atlantic in an airplane [1928] and the first woman to fly solo across the Pacific from Hawaii to California [1935]). Earhart set speed and distance records throughout her career and was active in many women's organizations. "Lady Lindy" became a beloved public figure partly through the promotional campaign engineered by her husband, George Putnam. In July of 1937, at age 40, Earhart was a month into an around-the-world flight when radio contact was lost in mid-Pacific, somewhere between New Guinea and tiny Howland Island. Despite numerous searches, her plane was never found.

Harriet Tubman was born into a slave family in Maryland in either 1820 or 1821. After she escaped to the North, she was determined to help her family and others flee slavery. As the best known conductor of the Underground Railroad, Tubman made some 19 trips to the South between 1850 and 1860, leading approximately 300 people to freedom. Her courageous exploits earned her the nickname "Moses." During the Civil War, she continued to work freeing slaves, and also aided the Union as a nurse, spy and military leader. After the war, she remained active for such causes as equality in education, women's suffrage and care of the sick and elderly.

Eleanor Roosevelt was an effective political and social leader in America. She was a staunch advocate of human rights worldwide and, in particular, championed the cause of women's and minority rights. Roosevelt organized many war-time relief activities and was also an effective political organizer for various causes on behalf of her husband's many campaigns. The mother of five children, her relationship with Franklin was never easy and yet their marriage endured. Eleanor's compassion for the plight and struggles of others propelled her to get involved with a wide range of social causes. Appointed as a delegate to the United Nations, Roosevelt played a major role in shaping the Universal Declaration of Human Rights, which passed in 1948.

Mother Teresa, whose original name was Agnes Gonxha Bojaxhiu, was born on August 27, 1910, in what is now Skopje, Macedonia. For her work with the poor around the world she received the 1979 Nobel Peace Prize.

In 1928, she joined a religious order and took the name Teresa. The order immediately sent her to India. A few years later, she began teaching in Calcutta, and in 1948 the Catholic Church granted her permission to leave her convent and work among the city's poor people. She became an Indian citizen that same year. In 1950, she founded a religious order in Calcutta called the Missionaries of Charity. The order provides food for the needy and operates hospitals, schools, orphanages, youth centers and shelters for lepers and the dying poor. It now has branches in 50 Indian cities and 30 other countries.

In addition to the 1979 Nobel Peace Prize, Mother Teresa received other awards for her work with the needy. These awards include the 1971 Pope John XXIII Peace Prize and India's Jawaharlal Nehru Award for International Understanding in 1972. Mother Teresa died on September 5, 1997.

I choose the poverty of our poor people. But I am grateful to receive [the Nobel] in the name of the hungry, the naked, the homeless, of the crippled, of the blind, of the lepers, of all those people who feel unwanted, unloved, uncared-for throughout society, people that have become a burden to the society and are shunned by everyone.

Mother Teresa

You Can Change the World

Women who change the world have learned how to have their hurts healed, how to live free of the past, and how to see themselves the way God sees them. They understand how to value themselves in God's plan, how to follow God's structure of integrity and character, and how to obey the Word of God. They have made a commitment to God and to themselves that they will not come to the end of themselves where they are, and that they will improve on their lives no matter what or how long it takes. Women who change the world know that they are a work in progress and that God is not through with them yet.

Woman of God, you have the ability to change the world. It has been in you since the beginning of creation until now. You've inherited the innate ability to wield

Women who change the world know
that they are a work in progress
and that God is not through with them yet.

power and influence, and you have the ability to make things happen.

Endnote

1. Kathryn Kuhlman, *I Believe in Miracles* (Old Tappan, NJ: Spire Books, 1969), 211, 216.

CHAPTER 9

A WOMAN OF INFLUENCE

Throughout history, women of influence have been criticized, shunned, disapproved, ignored and labeled for possessing the power and ability to impact their surroundings. But as any leader knows, criticism comes with the territory when you are in a position of power.

YOU HAVE BEEN CALLED TO LEAD

Leaders act with a sense of purpose, and they are passionate about their purpose. You have the traits of a leader, and you are called to lead others in the Kingdom. You are called to lead your husband and your children to Christ. You are called to minister and to comfort. You are called to change the world.

Following are ten traits of women leaders who are destined to change the world.

You have the ability to influence people. When you have the ability to influence people, you must be careful not to mislead people or abuse the power of your influence. As a woman of influence, God will hold you accountable for every word and every deed.

You have the ability to inspire others. The ability to inspire others means that you can tap into the deep emotional reserves of your life and share the joy of the Lord with others. You see the glass as half-full rather than half-empty and you can propel others to greatness through your actions.

You have the ability to direct others. I've often heard speakers quote, "When you teach a man, you educate an individual; but when you teach a woman, you educate a nation." A woman's ability to teach, to share and to direct others is a valuable gift. The ability to lead and direct others in the things of God is a blessing.

You have the ability to encourage people. The gift of encouragement is a lost art. We often are so self-absorbed that we neglect to see the needs of others. Women who change the world see past their own needs or desires and find within themselves the ability to encourage and support others.

Women who change the world see past
their own needs or desires and find within
themselves the ability to encourage and support others.

You have the ability to motivate others. A popular quote says, "Even if you're on the right track, you'll get run over if you just sit there." Women who change the world have the ability to motivate others. Whether it's through your words or your actions, the ability to compel others to move forward is a vital trait of leadership.

You have the ability to envision the future. If you don't know where you're going, how will you know when you get there? Leaders have the ability to plan ahead and envision the future. Women who change the world know that their vision comes from God and ultimately He is the One who directs their path.

You have the ability to make decisions. Many people fail because of their inability to make decisions. And in many cases, making no decision is a bad decision. Leaders—women who change the world—take decisive action and stick with their decisions. When you are firmly rooted in the Word and will of God, He will support your decisions.

You have the ability to mobilize others. An author once said, "I am more fearful of a herd of deer being led by a lion than a group of lions being led by a deer." Powerful and influential women mobilize people to act according to the standard they set.

You have the ability to anticipate change. In this life, change is the only thing that is constant. Leaders know that their past is not reflective of their future and that their present is subject to change. It is imperative that women of power and influence anticipate and accept change.

It is imperative that women of power
and influence anticipate and accept change.

You have the ability to be flexible and adaptable. A tree that bends and bows with the wind will become a great tree. A tree that refuses to bend will snap and break under the pressure. Leaders are flexible and adaptable.

THE IMPACT OF A WOMAN'S WORDS AND ACTIONS

How many times have we heard that actions speak louder than words? You influence the world by how you treat your husband, how your raise your children, how you honor your parents, how you respect your leaders, and how you represent your Father. Yes, it's true that people observe your actions, but they also remember the words you speak. Words are powerful. The Scriptures say that the power of life and death is in the tongue, and your words can sow seeds of kindness or cruelty, forgiveness or anger, healing or hurt.

As a woman of influence, your impact goes far beyond your own capabilities. It reaches down through generations by the legacy of your life. Your prayers reach heaven and change people's lives on earth. Your generosity improves the situations and circumstances of others. Your peace and joy encourage and minister to those in pain and in need of healing. Your life is a living testimony and influences countless individuals whom you may never meet. You must understand the depth of your ability to make a difference. Do not underestimate the difference that you make in the lives of others and the lessons that you can share.

AREAS OF INFLUENCE

There are several areas in the life of an influential woman that stand out and cause people to take notice:

1. Spiritual life and ministry.
2. Family life.
3. Health and lifestyle.
4. Attitude.
5. Inner/outer beauty.
6. Confidence.
7. Social/recreational life.
8. Career/professional life.
9. Financial life.
10. A balanced life.

Spiritual life and ministry. Everything in your life should reflect the goodness and the glory of God. Woman of influence, remember that you are made in the image of your Creator and your spiritual life is a reflection of the power and presence of God in your life. Your life may be the only Bible that some people ever read. A woman of influence understands that her spiritual foundation is the source and strength for everything else she attempts to do. And she is not afraid to let the world know who she is in Christ.

Family life. It can be a delicate balance to manage personal life and professional life and still keep both areas under control. However, no matter how busy our schedules are and how much attention our careers demand, we cannot overlook the importance of family. God gave us families as an extension of His love for us. Family is the core foundation of how we develop other relationships, and we must treat our family relationships as sacred.

There is no such thing as the perfect family; it's true that you can pick your friends, but you cannot pick your family. However, you must accept the family whom God has given you and nourish those relationships. The blood of family relationships, the strength of family ties and the love of adoption in family are all reflected in the Bible. Our family life can be a visual representation of the love of God for others to see. Even if you're a single woman, that doesn't mean you don't have family. Your relationships within your church and your community can be your family. And most importantly, your relationship with your Savior is the most important family bond in your life.

Health and lifestyle. A woman of influence knows that her body is the temple of God, the earthly residence for the Holy Spirit. How we treat our temple sends a message to others about how we honor the presence of God in our lives. It is not necessary to subscribe to the unreasonable and unrealistic standards of beauty that society has set, but it is a requirement that we honor the Lord in how we treat our bodies.

Attitude. How many times have you heard someone say that your attitude determines your altitude? Well, that's because it's true. You cannot go forward with a negative, defeated attitude and expect to come out with positive results. Your attitude and your countenance should be pleasant and inviting. No matter how strong the calling on your life or how many spiritual gifts you have, if you have a nasty attitude, you're dishonoring God and doing a disservice to His Kingdom. Your attitude should reflect the loving Spirit of Christ at all times. As a woman of influence, you never know who's watching you and who's observing how you handle various situations. You must remember that part of your responsibility as a woman of influence includes mentoring others and serving as a godly example of how to live.

Inner/outer beauty. Inner and outer beauty work hand in hand. The love, joy and peace that you have on the inside show up on the outside just like the frustration, stress and anxiety you have on the inside show up on your face, in your tone of voice and in the way you respond to others. No matter how many new clothes, or how much jewelry, perfume, lipstick and makeup you put on the outside, if the inner beauty isn't there, it's still a turn-off. A smile and a pleasant demeanor are the most attractive things a woman of influence can wear.

Confidence. Many women lack confidence for a variety of reasons. Millions of women are waiting on someone else's approval to build their confidence. Others are waiting on a man to tell them how beautiful they are, how desirable they are, how intelligent they are or how successful they are. Some still haven't healed from the abuses of their childhood or their past and cannot move on until those issues are resolved. And still there are some women who simply don't believe that they can be powerful and influential women in "a man's world." But a true woman of influence knows how to throw her own parade.

She knows that if nobody ever encourages her, or if nobody ever says something kind, that she is still who God said she is, and nobody can deny that. A woman of influence knows that it's not a man's world—it's God's world; that the "earth is the Lord's, and the fulness thereof; the world, and they that dwell therein" (Ps. 24:1 KJV). A woman of influence has God-confidence that allows her to sidestep the obstacles, let go of the past, learn from failures and defeat and walk on victoriously in Jesus' name.

Do not confuse confidence with arrogance. Confidence is knowing who you are in God. Arrogance is thinking that you somehow are responsible for your own success. A woman of influence is submitted to God, to her husband and to her spiritual leaders. A woman of influence is a servant to those in power and to those in need.

Social/recreational life. Someone once said, "Show me your friends, and I'll show you your future." A lifestyle based on all work and no play is not healthy—even for an anointed, powerful and influential woman of God. However, it's important to always be aware of your surroundings. You can't hang out in nightclubs, fill your mind with garbage, hang around with toxic people and still expect to flow in the Spirit of God.

Career/professional life. A woman of influence is a woman of integrity—even in the workplace. It is possible to be saved, sanctified and filled with the Holy Spirit and still be a CEO, president or vice president of a company. Just because you don't speak in tongues during your staff meetings doesn't mean the Spirit of God isn't residing with you and helping you to make godly decisions. We need more women of influence in corporate America to counteract some of the negative things we've been seeing on the news.

A woman of influence knows that God will promote her at the right time and that she doesn't have to sleep her way to the top or lie and cheat to get what she wants. She knows that God is her source and He will supply all of her need according to His riches in glory.

Financial life. For a long time, the Church confused poverty with spirituality and humility. The Church condemned having money because it was more spiritual to be poor. I'm here to tell you that the devil is a liar. Jesus died so that you might live. He became poor so that you could be rich. He came that you might have life, and that more abundantly. Do not believe that God does not want you to prosper and be successful. He wants you to be blessed so that you can bless others. God wants you to have wealth—which includes money—but He does not want riches and wealth to have you. A woman of influence has financial resources because she is tapped into the one true Source.

God wants you to have wealth—which
includes money—but He does not
want riches and wealth to have you.

A balanced life. The key here is to live a life of balance. You cannot excel in one area and fall short in all the others. I'm sure you've heard that some people are so heavenly minded that they're no earthly good. That's a good example of how being out of balance can do more harm than good. Life is not all spiritual, but it's not all natural either. Look to your Father, who is the author and the finisher of your faith, and He will guide you into a balanced life that glorifies Him.

How to Live a Non-Influential Life

There are ten practices that a woman of influence should not allow in her life:

1. Become a victim of your past.
2. Neglect to help others.
3, Become prideful as a result of your accomplishments.
4. Be defined by the opinions of others.
5. Repeat past mistakes.
6. Confuse the past with the present.
7. Confuse the present with the future.
8. Settle for less than God's best.
9. Live in false humility.
10. Allow anyone to dishonor the Spirit of God in your life.

Don't become a victim of your past. The past can be defined as the historic, immutable (unchangeable) spectrum of time that has already occurred. In other words, you can't fix it, so let it go. A woman of influence knows that she is a product of her past, her continual life experiences and her present environment. She recognizes that everyone—including herself—has made mistakes and done things that they regret. However, a woman of influence also recognizes the power of God in her life and respects His ability to mend and restore the broken pieces of the past. She recognizes that God is able to make all things work together for good for those who love God and are the called according to His purpose.

A woman of influence does not allow her past mistakes—or the mistakes of others—to disillusion her to the awesome possibilities in life. The past is merely a stepping stone and the training ground for a glorious future. As believers in Christ, we must accept the fact that dwelling on the past is a dangerous trap designed to ensnare and enslave us.

Nobody has a perfect past or perfect upbringing—not even Jesus. Indeed, Jesus was a perfect and upright man, but let's consider His genealogy and some of the members in His family. First, he was born to an unwed mother—in a stable—in a town that had a dismal reputation. Imagine what the townspeople must have said. Then consider who some of His ancestors were. Tamar was a victim of incest—a young woman who was raped by her own brother. Rahab is in the lineage of Jesus, and she was a prostitute. Ruth was an idol worshipper, Jacob was a cheat and a liar, and finally David was an adulterer. But Jesus overcame all those associations and stigmas and focused on doing His Father's will and fulfilling His divine purpose on earth. We too must be released from the past and welcome the opportunity to move forward.

Never neglect to help others. To some, it's very easy to look the other way and ignore the needs of others once they have "arrived." However, it is neither a reflection of power nor influence to fulfill our own desires while neglecting those who require our assistance. A woman of influence knows that her responsibilities lie outside her own household and into the far-reaching depths of the lives of others. A woman of influence knows that she cannot be oblivious to the cries of humanity and still consider herself successful.

Never become prideful. How many times have we heard the church mothers say something like, "If it had not been for the Lord on my side, I don't know where I'd be?" or, "Lord, we thank You for keeping us from dangers seen and unseen, because it could have been the other way," lest we forget that it is the Spirit of God who has kept us, protected us and provided for us through every trial, challenge and situation. It was the spirit of pride that introduced sin into the world, and pride has led to the downfall of humanity ever since. A woman of influence knows that she did not make it on her own.

A woman of influence knows
that she did not make it on her own.

Don't be defined by others' opinions. You do not have to be held hostage to somebody else's opinion of you. A woman of influence does not allow herself to be defined by others. Just because a thousand other people tried and failed does not mean that you will fail. Just because it's never been done before doesn't mean you aren't supposed to be the first one to do it. Just because we've

You are not defined by someone else's opinions of you.

never done it that way before doesn't mean there aren't opportunities for new ideas to arise and break forth. Just because you look just like your alcoholic mother, or your addicted sister, or your unsaved aunt, doesn't mean you can't live a life that's holy and pleasing to God. Your first and foremost priority is to live a life that's pleasing to the Father. You are not defined by someone else's opinions of you.

Learn from past mistakes. A popular definition of insanity is "doing the same thing and expecting different results." It is true that God's grace is sufficient, but He does expect us to learn from our mistakes and to not keep repeating the same thing over and over again. I often say that good judgment comes from experience, and experience comes from bad judgment. If you can't learn from your mistakes, there's no point in making them. A woman of influence knows that all eyes are upon her and people will respond to how she handles trials and adversity. Unfortunately, people may lose confidence in their own abilities if they see one of God's leaders repeatedly struggling with the same issue year after year. You are a light—an example to the world—so use your mistakes as springboards into the next phase of your life and as testimonies to the goodness of God's grace and mercy.

Don't confuse your past and present. Women of God, leaders, pastors, homemakers, ministers, businesswomen and mothers: Don't confuse the past with the present or confuse the present with the future. A lot of people won't pursue their dreams or step out on faith because they've failed before. They think that what is now is what will always be, and that simply isn't the case. You are a different person today than you were ten years ago, a year ago or a month ago. Each experience in life gives us an opportunity to learn, grow and develop into the person God has destined us to be. The past is not indicative of your future if you want to change for the better. And don't mistakenly think that your present circumstances are indicative of your future. Once again, what is now is not what will always be.

Have you ever heard the phrase, "What a difference a day makes"? Well, if things can change in a moment, how many more opportunities will you have in the future to reach your goals and fulfill your dreams? A woman of influence will absolutely not allow her past or present circumstances dictate her future.

A woman of influence will absolutely
not allow her past or present
circumstances dictate her future.

Never settle for less than God's best. It is a tragedy how many powerful and influential women of God will live an unfulfilled life, die and be buried with all of their talents and gifts. I'm amazed at how often women are willing to settle for less because they think that's all they deserve. That is a lie straight out of hell—orchestrated by the devil to rob you of your future.

A woman of influence knows that God has her best interest at heart and that anything less than God's best is unacceptable. She knows that she doesn't have to submit her life and future to a man who doesn't appreciate her, who doesn't have a job and who mistreats her. A woman of influence is not afraid to be alone because she knows that it's better to be alone than in bad company. A woman of influence will not allow herself to be mentally and physically abused by a man because that's the best she can do—she's willing to wait on God.

Women of influence know that their value is worth more than a physical relationship with a man who doesn't love them. She knows her body is the temple of God and dishonoring it devalues her worth. She knows that it takes more than one night to get to know someone. Real women of power and influence understand that God doesn't do things halfway. God won't send her a man she has to fix or a job that compromises her integrity. Women of influence realize that some things are worth waiting for. Honor your mind, your body and your spirit. Know that God created you to be first and not last, the head and not the tail. Know that God doesn't want you to settle for less.

➤   ◄

**A woman of influence knows
that God has her best interest at heart
and that anything less than God's best is unacceptable**

➤────────────◄

Don't live in false humility. There's a fine line between modesty and false humility. It is wonderful to see powerful and influential women walking in humility. But it's very sad to see them so unconvinced of their own worth that they cannot even accept a compliment. There are people who simply do not believe they are worthy of other people's thanks or appreciation. That is not modesty— that's false humility. God wants you to recognize who you are in Him. The most appropriate way to accept a genuine compliment is to say, "Thank you." Do not lead a life of false humility. Walk in modesty and let your life glorify God.

Finally, don't allow anyone to dishonor the Spirit of God in your life. Some people will literally drain the life out of you if you let them. They never have anything positive to say, and they aren't encouraging you to meet your goals.

Do not allow yourself to be a conduit (channel) for negative energy. Gossiping is one of the top ways to attract negative energy. Lying and complaining are right up there at the top also. These habits are huge time and energy wasters and serve no positive purpose. Entertaining this type of behavior grieves the Holy Spirit and dishonors His presence in your life.

GOD CREATED YOU TO BE A WOMAN OF POWER AND INFLUENCE

It's time to take inventory of your life and consider whether or not you are a woman of power and influence. How are you using that power? Are you using it to deceive, control, dominate or manipulate? Or are you using it to share the gospel and pave the way for others? Who are you influencing and what are you influencing them to do? Are you a good role model for your children, your friends and your coworkers? Is God pleased with the example you're setting? Remember, to whom much is given, much is required.

Our God is a God of purpose, and He has a purpose for you in mind. As a woman, you are of great worth and value to God, and whatever He has called you to do, you will be able to accomplish in the name of Jesus.

Your time has come! Whether you are called by God to pray for your neighborhood, support and provide for your family, serve as a leader in your church or business, or impact the entire world, you've been given divine authority to make a positive difference for the Kingdom of God. You are a woman of power and influence!

MINISTRY INFORMATION

Kingsley Fletcher Ministries
P.O. Box 12017
Research Triangle Park, NC 27709-2017

Phone: 919-382-1944
Fax: 919-382-3360

Website: www.kfmlife.org